LILAC CITY FAIRY TALES

Marry a Monster

PUBLISHED BY SCABLANDS BOOKS

Edited by Sharma Shields and Ellen Welcker
Cover illustration by John Rawley
Book design by Keely Honeywell

"Conceit" previously appeared in the *Hawai'i Pacific Review* and is reprinted here with permission.
"The Idea" by Simeon Mills originally appeared in *Pinch Journal*.

Printed in Spokane by Gray Dog Press

You have to fight magic with magic. You have to believe
That you have something impossible up your sleeve...

The will to do whatever must be done:
Marry a monster. Hand over your firstborn son.

From the poem, "Fairy-tale Logic"
BY A. E. STALLINGS

TABLE OF CONTENTS

Lilac City Fairy Tales: Marry a Monster

GINGER GREY

How to marry a monster
(in six easy steps)

1 First, ask yourself the tough questions: Why do you want to marry a monster? For the prestige? The adventure? The company? Are you perhaps a monster yourself? What kind of monster really does it for you? A cyclops? A dragon-man? A narcissist? A demon? And how far would you move for love? To another planet? Under the ocean? To hell?

2 Once you've clarified your own assumptions and needs, it's time to find your monster-spouse! There are so many places to look. The bar. The internet. You are bound to meet a monster at a lecture on sustainability. Try the galleries, attend a seminar on happiness. Go places monsters like to hang out: inside dark warehouses, hollowed-out trees, your mother's skull.

3 Initiate an introduction! Tell the monster two or three things about yourself, and then forget you are a person. Ask a lot of questions, and when the monster makes a joke, laugh gently while touching his arm / horn / boil. Above all: admire the monster. Be like his mother. Be like his sympathetic and ineffectual therapist. Be like the voice inside his head that tells him he can stop killing children at any time.

4 If he is warm-blooded, be warm. If he is cold-blooded, be the sun on a July day in Calcutta.

5 And when the monster says / growls / writes in blood on the last page of your gratitude journal, "I will destroy you," tell him you are not afraid. And mean it. Do not try to bring the undead back to life. Do not file any antlers, or bleach any scales. Do not, even in your sleep, wish for fewer heads.

6 The night before the wedding, accept your death. It may come quickly: a ritual at the close of your big church ceremony. Or it may take years: a decade of fire-breathing, a lifetime of tiny, mean jabs. But look at you. You are beautiful. You are kind. Any monster would be lucky to strip the flesh from your determined, magnificent bones.

MAYA JEWELL ZELLER

A Narrow Dress

Therianthropy: the man becomes
the beast. A woman's flesh
unfolds to reveal a skirt of thorns.

Her skirt unfolds to reveal fire.
Her fire rips at the door.
Her door opens, a beast

leaps onto the page. The sheets
peel back like skin, we're in
the bed, he and I, a skirt

of horns. What is borne
in the brain becomes
bone. What strains at its ropes

is my brain. Therianthropy,
they say, is my desire
to be animal. *That* isn't it.

Have you ever looked so hard
through leaves they all become
eyes? Have your eyes

grown leaves in their looking?
I like to make leaf-art.
I layer them, one on another.

What does this look like
to you? Can you smell fear
on my breath? The beast

turns female. She pulls
her heavy body across
the beach. She finds herself

in a city of thorns, torn
open, her bones open,
her sparrow homes,

her song of leaves.
Her fired skirt.
Her small, smoldering dress.

MAYA JEWELL ZELLER

She Dreams of Children

You say marrow   I say dress
marrow   dress
marrow   dress

You say cephalopod
I say triceratops

You change colors faster than a chameleon
while scientists debate over my horns and frills
and I wear my face to prom
my prom of the three horned face

I promenade at prom while you scrape your bones
along the floor. This floor is made of bones.
This floor is home. This floor is home.

You jump out the window into the ocean
where every seventh wave crashes whiter to the right
along the ropes we've set out to measure them

and you can hold the rope with one of your eight arms
and I can face the window with my three horns

and they can make my face a tiara
and your arms a dress

that clings to bone.

You say marrow   I say dress
marrow   dress
marrow   dress

You say squid I say marry
squid   marry
squid   marry

Nautilus   cuttlefish   octopus

I want to die   I want to die in your eight arms
and be carried into the bone floor
your bone floor
your floor of bones
your arms of lace
facing me in my tight white dress

NATALIE PEETERSE

Grendel's Girl

Oh, heart of ancient thunder, oh heart of drunk bloodlust—
it is easy for me to see why they are so afraid of you—
afraid to love that terrible heart, its lakes of fire
and loops of rain, the mist and fog of its slopeland.
This way and that way you stagger and they scatter.
I wish they could hear below the roar
: a belligerent longing for poetry.

Oh, you, who loves you?
How hard it is to watch you parade the shores of the gore
you inflict while you wait and wait for the stars to align—
and for the words to come—and they never quite do.
We have to live in that space in between :
what we want and what we get. Nothing left to do
but to raid our lessers as they roam the scrublands,
searching for their own answers, or just surviving.
All things are just in sight : just out of sight.

Oh, love. My love for you flickers in and out : on and off
: like starlight leaking through the pools of mud and dread
and the hoops of fire to our home at the bottom of all things.
To land on your face when you finally sleep.
We can always look up and dream, can't we?
We can swim up and search together—scour everywhere—
for that one Shaper worth saving

DENNIS HELD

The Butterfly, the Limousine

It's one of those bad-idea weddings
where the groom is drunk by noon
and the bride's crying under her veil.
Everybody knows the marriage is doomed
but nobody cares: our marriages failed
years before but that's no reason to split.
After the you-may-kiss-the-bride, the groom's
fat tongue and mugging, we all go outside
with our very own pastel cardboard box
and a live butterfly inside. When I let mine go—
Be free, little one!—a sparrow hawk
snatches it midair before my eyes. Whap!
Then comes thunder, hard rain, and forty throbbing
butterflies knocked to the street, under the limousine.

J. ROBERT LENNON

Whiskey

When he comes home, she is sitting on the sofa, holding a bottle of whiskey.

I've decided to try drinking, she says.

Drinking? he asks her. Why?

We're complacent. Blandly happy. It's time for a change.

We're not happy at all, he says.

I'm sick of everything being comfortable and easy, she says, taking a deep swig from the bottle. I'm shaking things up.

Things are very hard, he says. We live in an environment of complete emotional chaos.

Don't you want a little risk in your life? she says. A little drama? There's no drama around here, she says, drinking.

No, I don't. I don't want any drama.

Have some, she says, offering him the bottle.

No, he says. He's still standing by the door, in his running sneakers, holding a briefcase.

It's vile. Seriously. It cost eight dollars.

Are you drunk yet? he asks.

Yes.

Do you like it?

That's not the point, she says. The point is that alcohol ruins lives. I'm trying to bring ruin down upon us. Eight dollars is a small price to pay for that.

We've been ruined for some time, he observes.

He goes to the bedroom, takes off his shoes, and lies down. He reads some things on the internet about coping with an alcoholic spouse. Then he watches some videos about ghosts, and some videos of people falling down and getting hit by things. He looks at some pictures of girls' breasts. He hears her climbing the stairs and entering the bathroom, and then he hears the sound of vomiting.

He gets up off the bed, goes into the bathroom, and sits on the floor beside her. The room reeks of cheap booze. It's the smell of ruined lives. He pats her on the back as she throws up.

Stop that, she says. It's annoying.

I love you very much, he says.

It's not me you love, she says, wiping snot and saliva from her face, and gazing blearily into his eyes. It's my sickness.

J. ROBERT LENNON

Pie

She says, What are you doing?

She has just walked into the kitchen. He is concentrating on something at the counter. It is clear by his posture that it isn't going well. He says, Nothing.

You are not doing nothing, she says. You've got a bowl and some flour there. And butter. You've got a bunch of fruit.

I see a cookbook.

You're cooking, she summarizes.

No, I'm not.

You are cooking, she says. Then she adds, You don't cook.

His shoulders twitch. He turns to look at the cookbook, revealing his face. It is tight and flushed.

After a while, he says, I am baking.

You don't bake, she says.

Well, it looks like you're wrong, he says.

She sits at the table. She takes out her phone and uses it to ignore him. Every few minutes, he emits a quiet oath.

She laughs at something on her phone.

Look! she says. She holds up the phone.

He turns. His forehead is dripping sweat. He wipes it away with his shirtsleeve, which is also sweaty.

On the phone's screen, an animal is doing something funny.

That's funny, he says, unsmiling, and returns to his work.

So, she says, putting the phone away. Why the fuck are you baking?

For fun, he says.

You're not having fun, she says. You're miserable.

So what if I am, he says.

If you suck at it, and it's not fun, what's the point?

He mutters a reply, too quiet to hear.

What? she says. Speak up.

I said, I was reading an article about marriage.

What does that have to do with anything? Marriage? What?

He grunts. A little cloud of flour rises up from the counter. He says, The article says you can make your husband happy by baking him a pie. So I'm baking you a pie.

You're the husband, you asshole, she says. I'm the wife.

Whatever, he says. The principle is the same. You're unhappy, so I'm baking a pie.

I'm not fucking unhappy, she says. Who said I was?

He doesn't answer. After a while she returns to chuckling at her phone. When, some time later, the sound of quiet sobbing reaches her from the counter, she puts the phone away and goes to him.

She says, You're doing it wrong.

No, I'm not.

Yes you are.

I've got the butter and the flour. And the sugar. And I'm putting them together and it's just a...it's crap. It's a ball of fucking crap.

Move.

No.

Don't be a baby, she says. Move over.

He steps aside, but not quite enough. She pushes him with her hip. He stumbles with an exaggerated motion.

This butter is warm, she says. You need cold butter. And ice water. Where's the fucking ice water?

Ice water? he says.

For fuck's sake, she says.

She throws everything he has done away. Then she spends forty minutes clanking around in the kitchen, making a pie.

She makes a crust and then she makes the filling and then she puts more crust on top of the filling and she puts the pie into the oven. During this time he retreats to the table and sits very still, with his head on his crossed arms.

When she joins him at the table, clapping the excess flour from her hands, he abruptly gets up, his chair clattering to the floor behind him. He runs from the room. A moment later, a distant door slams.

When the pie is ready, she takes it out of the oven, cuts a piece, and puts it on a plate. She brings it up to the bedroom. But the door is locked.

Open the fucking door, she says.

No.

I brought your pie.

I don't like pie, he says, his voice muffled by what sounds like a pillow.

Of course you do, she says. Everybody likes pie.

I don't like hot fruit.

You don't like what? What kind of fucking phobia is that?

I didn't say I was afraid of it, he says, more clearly now. I said I didn't like it.

Baking makes the husband happy, she says. I'm setting it down here in the hallway, and you better fucking eat it. I spent a fucking hour baking it for the sake of our marriage. You're going to grow up and eat it and it's going to make you happy. If I come up here in fifteen minutes and I don't see an empty plate outside this door, I'm going to break in there and fucking force-feed you marriage therapy. Do you understand?

He doesn't answer. She goes downstairs, serves herself a piece of pie, and laughs at funny animals on her phone while eating it.

Meanwhile, upstairs, the door opens a crack and a hand snakes out. It drags the plate of pie through the opening. The door closes.

A few minutes later, the sounds of crying can be heard, followed by the sounds of eating.

TIM GREENUP

Drinks with Sam

Green liquid burbles from the porous
dark red walls of a small cave pulsing
inside my friend Sam, who is seated
across from me but is also drowning
in one of North Idaho's cold lakes,
his pant leg snagged on the periscope
of a submarine going down, down,
deep, down to silently implode and be forgotten
like a man. I buy him another beer and
say "cheer up, buddy." The green liquid churns.
He tells of his high school cheerleader
love who wrapped her Jeep around a tree
and spent prom night alone dying. Her lungs
ballooned with her own blood, he weeps.
He begins to munch on his pint glass
as if it were rock candy, and I know
he will soon cough up an emerald, and
hand it to me, saying "give this to your wife,"
before slinking back behind the ice maker
for another year of wet and troubled sleep.

TIM GREENUP

A Scene

The horizontal woman moves
into me. The ceiling dips and
presses our bodies, draining
them, like tofu on a countertop.
The mattress sops. We cannot
stop crying but keep breathing.
We're in a bad way. Over the hill
the castle waits for the fog
to take it back. A groundskeeper
outside the cemetery gates hears
a sudden hollow moaning.

TIM GREENUP

Becoming Jeff Lebowski

Drowning vodka
with milk and mocha, we
bowl on the Asiatic rug. We
impregnate pale, red-eyed women.
It's a life. We cherish it, but
never forget the Germans –
techno music and grandeur looming.
Who knows what they'll do?
The Rapture happened.
Airplanes crashed
into the East; we wait
for the sky to split and
dump ash on everything.
One more reason to eat a burger
while watching pornography. Outside, everyone
wears sandwich-boards, faces greased,
hollering *Nigh! Nigh! The End is Nigh!*
From rooftops, gargoyles
wash the city.
Below, some kid
gathers every gold coin,
walks to the fridge, steps inside,
and immolates.

ELLEN WELCKER

Nature Poem

Let's say you're a female animal
and a parasite has infected your brain,
made you do crazy things. Let's say
it's not living inside you, exactly,
but near you, near enough to come
inside you, dripping poison,
though let's say it's not poison,
but a magic elixir that mixes
with yours, begins to grow. See
how out of control things
can be? Let's say you're not
a woman, exactly, but female,
a female animal, and someone,
another animal, wants to nest
inside you. She looks around
for someplace to get in and
when she does, she leaves her body
behind: now she has yours.
Her nest might look like a tumor
hip-checking for wiggle room, hungry
for your food. The animal renders
your sex organs useless and you care
for the children of this shadow-you. How
she bores a hole in you: makes a new
vagina, where they can come
to mate with her through you,
an animal, too.

KISHA LEWELLYN SCHLEGEL

The Veil

In the years behind our years, there was a woman who didn't need a wedding day to wear a veil. Julia Pastrana had a husband. He took her from town to town. He showed her where to sleep and where to stand. He showed her how to hide her marketable face from a public that had not yet paid. This was the configuration of his world. To go anywhere, she would have to cover up. She would wear a veil.

Under the veil, in every city, she passed through crowds made of eyes. The boys stopped slinging their pebbles. The men buttoned their topcoats closer to the neck. Women tried to gasp through the tight-laced corsets worn in London that year. 1857. They registered her difference. Her dark skin. Her thick eyebrows. The new moon dark of her eyes. The veil. The veil moved with the person it enclosed. Like wind in a sail, it moved with a hidden force, one that could move a body across oceans if charted by the stars.

Those who didn't see beyond the veil, would have to pay three shillings to get off on her face. They would have to come to the theater and commit to the act of watching her. They would have to wed their monster vision and refuse to say human. Woman. This was a time of spectacle. Of P.T. Barnum and Human Zoos. Of "Miss Julia Pastrana" who stood on their stage, so they could view the "Marvelous Hybrid" that the posters had promised. "Monkey Woman." "Bear Woman." "From the jungle," said the pamphlets even though she was from the mountains of the Sierra Madre in Mexico, born to a tribe who saw the black beard covering her face and cried out *naualli*, wolf, shape-shifter, half-human, currency.

Her uncle sold her to a traveling circus. The circus sold her to the governor. The governor made the rules of the household that kept her.

He made her his entertainment and maid. Still, she learned to read. She learned to speak Spanish. English. At twenty she ran away.

On the road, she met a man on a horse. He rode high toward conquest. Mr. Rates. An American. He took her. He sold her to Mr. Lent, who married her to make sure she was never sold to anyone else.

There would be no domesticity in the small hotel rooms. She was checked in and out. Her private door opened to those who paid an extra fee. She wore the veil until her husband arrived. It was only then that she would remove it to let them locate the shining hair of her beard, hanging down below her chin.

Their investigation of her beard led to her mouth, which she opened for each of them so they might view and try to catalog the absence of certain teeth, the presence of unexpected ones.

"Breasts," one wrote. "She has the parts of a woman entire." Of her hair, the doctors said: "Opaque, straight, not Negroid but something else altogether." Something else. Something "animal. Hybrid. Baboon. Ourang Outang. Bear. Bear-Woman. The Misnomered. The Nondescript," as in that which has not yet been described.

When the curtain opened, Julia wore no veil. A single body constellated animal and human.

The crowd didn't know how to see what they didn't know to see.

First came the fear of the growing desire to do more than look at her—to touch her and touch that which could not be described. Then came the growing awareness that she might not recoil from this touch. She might hover closer, close enough to lift the gaze between them and expose to them the question they were too afraid to ask: Am I you?

She stood before them in small black shoes. She wore a velvet dress of her own making. With a "well-turned ankle" she danced the Highland Fling. She sang in a mezzo-soprano, "The Last Rose of Summer." She surprised them with her ability to speak. To speak English. To speak Spanish. She surprised them with her ability. Her 4′ 6″ body stood in for the conversation no one would have. By the end of the night, she had completed the impossible task: she stood in the space of their fear. And sang. She sang into the silence of being watched.

By Moscow, Julia's husband didn't let her walk outside at all. She wasn't allowed to walk through the churchyard or lay her body down. Still, she knew star-rise. She knew moon-rise. The moon was a fine, toothed dragon with a soft stone of a heart. It bit through the dark fog of every city, past the gray buildings, the charred edges of the chimneys, past the confines of every structure and toward this sister-star, whose powers of body and mind were strangely wasted, dispersed, forgotten—whose powers flashed here and there like falling stars and died before the world would rightly gauge their brightness. [Du Bois]

By Moscow she was pregnant. She delivered a boy with a beard like hers and hair that radiated down his soft back. For thirty-five hours she shared his life. She held him beneath the star-children and the twinkling lights as they began to flash and stilled with an even-song the unvoiced terror of this life. [Du Bois]

When the baby died, her husband sold tickets to her deepest suffering. Spectators came to look at Julia in her hospital bed and still did not see. Three days later she was dead. Her husband sold the body of the child and the body of Julia to a doctor who embalmed them. He stood them upright. He bolted their feet to parallel rods and enclosed them in a glass case.

They traveled for more than a hundred years, displayed around Europe and America and ultimately stashed in a Norwegian warehouse. There, a group of boys broke in and pulled off an arm they saw as a mannequin. They lost the baby's body in another field of disfigurement from which it could not be recovered.

It took an artist to repatriate Julia and bury her in Sinaloa de Leyva, Mexico, under a tombstone that reads: Artist. Music played. Inside the coffin are garments ceremonial to her tribe and a photograph of her child on her chest. Someone removed the bolts from her feet and placed them at the end of the casket. They closed the lid. They lifted the body into the plane which rose to take her home under a new moon.

That was a time that is here now.

When it is dark to us, the new moon doesn't hang behind the shadow of this earth as so many people believe. It hovers between the earth and the sun. What appears dark to us is illuminated. It too shines with a light we can't see. It's being beautiful belongs to nothing. [Notley]

AMARIS FELAND KETCHAM

Tiger Salamander
Ambystoma tigrinum

On the backside of the mountain, the man cut wood and the woman
wove every day. He had thick, sturdy legs. The man hunted
and the woman collected fresh sprigs of rosemary and dug yucca
roots. She worked at night and didn't mind the mud. The man was
terrestrial and loyal to his birthplace. The woman made tonics
from nearby blossoms—coneflower for a cold, aster for gingivitis,
honeysuckle for nostalgia. She often asked the man for different water,
with other minerals suspended. Some ponds had a metallic taste.
Some, a hint of mouse droppings, or a weird aroma, *à la* India,
1963. Some might have new curative powers.

He searched for puddles made in the monsoon rains, and one night
found fresh, still water. His face reflected in the pool, duplicated
with the moon, vivid black and yellow ripples. He drank; an irreversible
smile worked his lips. He felt new and strong. This was the fountain of youth!
Before returning home, he dug his hands into muddy banks and pulled
out a night crawler, which he ate.

A young man has no want of an old woman. She should hurry
to the monsoon pool that turned back time. Together they could be forever
juvenile. She hitched her skirts and rushed in the direction of the water.
He waited; the moon breached its apex, passed through papery clouds,
and he grew concerned. He went to the woman, but the path
was difficult. Each step took a long time.

When he approached the pool, he saw she had indeed grown younger.
Her skin was a youthful, murky cream dotted with dark green. She smiled
broadly across her wide jaw. As she swam, feathery gills waved in the water
and tail fins guided her this way and that. She had drank too much,
reentered her larval state. His neotenic gal. His baby eft. She was
aquatic now, and he did not know if she would mature enough to ever walk
on land again. He dug a shallow pool for her near their burrow
as the August sun climbed a clear, blue sky.

ELIN HAWKINSON

House of the Three White Roses

Snow was falling on the Charles Bridge. Large clumps formed on the still shoulders of St. Wenceslaus, St. John, the Madonna. Christ in his lamentations. Lone flakes danced in the air before disappearing forever into the Elbe. The world was black and white: dark wools, pale sky, sooty stone. A hundred wild swans.

I rested my arms on the balustrade and watched the swans paddle through the murky water, bobbing with the waves brought on by sudden gusts of an icy wind. Swans had been creatures of myth in my dry Midwestern childhood. Yet here they were, so many as to seem common, squabbling and chivvying amongst themselves like my old fat aunts around my grandmother's kitchen table.

My husband took my mittened hand and pulled me along with the rest of our tour group. It was Christmas Eve. We were treating ourselves to an outing, not saying aloud how tired we were of winter, of being foreigners, of scraping by on bread rolls and milk while my husband finished a graduate degree in Kafka studies. In late Autumn Prague had been like a storybook city, but now it was chill and wet and grim. Home seemed very far away.

The tour began at a ruined castle where a servant girl had been beaten to death after pleading with her mistress to be allowed to go to mass. Then we passed the foundation of a building where it was said an orphan child had been buried alive to appease the devil. Beneath the Old Town Square lay the ancient catacombs of Prague, and beneath the catacombs, according to legend, lay hell.

We stood now before an old mansion. Three white roses had been carved above the door. The house once belonged to three sisters, the tour guide said, each bright and beautiful as the sun. Every afternoon they could be seen by the townspeople sitting in their bedroom windows, combing their long golden hair. Each in her turn was wooed and won by a mysterious prince, who swept her and her vast fortune far away from Prague. When the last sister had been married and carried off, the townspeople wiled away the dull hours imagining their glorious fates. But not long afterward a stranger—cloaked in blackest velvet—rode into town and stopped at the inn for a drink and supper. When he heard the tale he laughed.

There were not three *princes*, said the man. *There was only* one. *The greatest prince of any land. After he married them he carried them only to the outskirts of the city, where he put them to death and left them to rot, their fortunes safe in his hand.*

The townspeople were angry. They would not listen to such spiteful gossip against the favored daughters of Prague. *How can you be certain*, they asked him, *that what you say is true?*

Because I am him, the stranger said, throwing back his hood and cloak so that all might see his terrible face. The townspeople cowered in fear.

"It was Lucifer, Prince of Darkness," our tour guide concluded, smiling too broadly. Then he removed his top hat and bowed.

While my husband picked through the few coins in his pocket for a tip, I wondered what could be so terrible about the face of Satan. Ugliness? Disfigurement? Eyes fireball red? It didn't make sense to me that he could have deceived three women unless he was handsome, charming. I'd known plenty of women to fall for just such a snare.

Tour over, we walked away from the crowded square. The snow came harder now—no longer feathers but stinging chips of ice. My husband looked for a pub, but it was late afternoon and doors were already beginning to close. Down a side street we found a little bar with only three tables. The lamps were still lit so we went in and sipped at twin glasses of Urquell, pretending they were dinner.

"Kafka had three sisters," my husband said after awhile. He chewed at the nail on his right thumb, making a clicking sound.

"I didn't know that," I said. Though I did. But I wanted my husband to talk to me, the way he had before he was always exhausted, and I was always pinched and worried and careful not to look too far ahead.

"They died in the camps."

We sat there until the bartender noisily began to put on his coat and over-boots. My husband stopped chewing at his nail and we both saw how it had been bitten down to the quick.

Outside in the cold, I asked my husband if we could walk back across the Charles Bridge so I might look at the swans again. Through the snow-swirled darkness I could make out a great flock of them huddled together around the piles for warmth—impossible to tell where one bird left off and another began.

We left Prague a year later. My husband won a teaching position at a worthwhile university. I took work as a nursery school aide. Before long we had children and there were other things to talk about. Prague was cast as a youthful lark—dinner party conversation. How young we had been. How silly and quaint.

Yet once in a while, with the children at the zoo or park, I remember the swans. Their double arrogance of loveliness and perfection—I have never encountered it since. But as there is beauty in symmetry there is beauty in aberration. Pompeii. Bombed-out cathedrals. Rusted, curling wire. Clouds. Two people together and still so alone. A swan—or a snowflake—pales in comparison to such distortion of form and purpose.

And over the years, I happened across other accounts of the story of the three beautiful sisters. Sometimes they had an old nurse woman who watered the ground with her tears, and from the same ground sprung a white rose bush. Sometimes the youngest sister escaped the prince and fled to the snowy Krkonoše Mountains, where she became a good witch and aided those lost in the pass. In another version, my favorite, the sisters turned themselves into swans and flew away from the prince, leaving dolls of straw in their places.

KIMBERLY KENT

Baba Yaga's Lover

I came of my own freewill to kiss
her bony-legs, to build a fire
in the red clay stove, to lay
a blanket on a bed
of bones for us, to hang herbs
from the mouths of the men
whose skulls adorn her
fireplace. I came to press
my cheek, then my bare breasts
to her hollow face, lay my body next
to her body— whisper *laziness*
grief, death into her angular
ear—her house dancing slowly
through the woods beneath us.

I love her black hair tied-up
in a red hanker-chief, but what I love
most is how she runs through the rye fields
with her hair loose like a shadow
trailing her—everywhere
and nowhere.

After I make a home of her
house I no longer wish
to be mistress to a witch, so we wed.
That day my eyes are bluer than eggs
and I too am dressed in the forest:
like bark from an old spruce tree.

And soon by my own fairy-tale logic—
this mysterium of plot— I can no longer
tell who I was. I am Baba Yaga
and my wife is Baba Yaga and we
are Baba Yaga. A clash
of iron-teeth. The body
is such a foolish thing. We grow
slow and bald and leave
our old skin behind us as we go.

Now one hand stirs the pot, one hand
pushes the mop. One mouth cries out
through the woods. Sorry if we've
scared your dog.

Some days we face each other
and other days I say: fuck it.
Look at this fence I've built.
Look at all these smooth bones.
Look how white they are.
Look how white they turn in the sun.

ELI FRANCOVICH

META

Watching her eat meat reinforced the gravity of my mistake.

She's stuffing her face. Sure, it's just salmon, but fish are friends, too.

I'm a vegan. I have a card. I'm certified. She knows this. She's folded my "I heart vegetables" shirt. I was very honest, very upfront about my political beliefs and socially conscious environmentally positive life habits.

She lied to me. She's a lying carnivorous cow.

"Would you like some more wine?" she asks. If you didn't know better you'd think nothing was wrong.

She is sweet. She's a gentle, caring woman. We've been married for nearly six months. In the morning she brings me coffee.

Finding the good in people, and situations, is a key component of my philosophy.

But, it's been a long day and our marriage is wearing thin. Right now, as she chews on some brutalized animal, all I can see are her transgressions.

We met at a vegan dinner. Well, to be fair, I hosted the dinner and all my dinners are vegan–so perhaps it wasn't specifically a vegan dinner.

I was smitten. She moved so gracefully.

When we first started dating she didn't eat meat, or at least I never saw her eat meat. I assumed, incorrectly, that she was vegan.

"Hey, Brian, babe, would you stop kissing me if I ate fish occasionally?" She asked one evening, one month after we were married.

I almost said yes, but then I realized she wasn't joking.

"No, just brush your teeth afterward?"

Somewhere, back in my educational past, I learned that the "slippery slope" argument is a fallacy.

I wholeheartedly disagree. The occasional fish led to the weekly fish, the weekly fish to the occasional chicken, the occasional chicken to the regular chunk of cow. She said it was about body type and blood sugar, the usual excuses.

I tried. I really did. I burned incense and donated more money than ever to various vegan causes, but I never brought it up with her because, I realize now, I was scared.

Sitting in this restaurant watching her eat, I don't know that I can stand it any longer. I feel that I must make a point, a stand for what's right. I can't be scared any longer.

She licks her lips as if in an effort to prolong the homicidal enjoyment. Monster.

I don't believe she's innately bad. Instead I prefer to think she's a victim of bad life habits.

Monster.

"Do you have to do that?" I can't hold back any longer. As I speak I point at her bloody plate. A Brussels sprout is neatly speared on my fork. No blood. No torture.

"Do what?"

"Eat living, sentient beings."

She frowns.

"Brian, what are you talking about?"

"You know exactly what I'm talking about." I raise my voice, nearly swearing, but I stop myself. As a rule, I try to avoid verbal violence.

"The meat? We talked about this."

I slam my fist down. The restaurant goes quiet. Everyone is anticipating my vengeful retribution.

"You're. Eating. MEAT."

With each word I point my fork, Brussels sprout neatly speared, at her.

"Brian, calm down."

"Don't condescend to me!"

I'm standing now.

Everyone in the restaurant is staring, their mouths agape, transfixed by my display of moral fortitude–my stand against the oppression and destruction of innocence.

"Baby." She's trying to calm me down. But this time I won't let her.

She's half standing, her chair scooted back. She's flushed. No doubt she's realizing the gravity of her sin.

"Brian, not again, not here…."

"Don't…" I'm warning her. I may be an herbivore, but I can be ferocious when threatened.

Socially conscious and environmentally friendly ferocity.

Now I'm shaking. I need to amplify this. Make a stand for the voiceless. A cry for the downtrodden.

I'm still brandishing the fork with the speared Brussels sprout. As I prepare my next point I spastically snap my wrist, releasing the green missile toward my wife.

A year later that moment remains fresh in my memory.

I've lost a lot of weight in prison. The vegan options are slim.

When I flung the Brussels sprout I missed my wife. Instead, the little green innocent lodged itself deep in the throat of an elderly gentleman who was watching—with his mouth agape. He started choking, and in the chaos of waiters and patrons trying to remove me from the restaurant and my wife pleading with them not to call the cops, no one noticed that he'd collapsed.

When the Brussels sprout was finally dislodged, he'd been without air for roughly eight minutes; he went into a coma and died the next day. He was old, so I figured I'd get off easy. Maybe do a little community service.

I was wrong. I'm six months into a three-year sentence. Second degree manslaughter.

I've said it before, it's difficult living among meat eaters.

The thing is, and I've thought about this a lot, I was right when I confronted her. It would have been better if the old man hadn't died, but there are always unintended casualties in a war.

And that's what this is. A war for what's right. A war for justice, peace. A war to reclaim our collective humanity.

That's my story. My name is Brian and I'm a socially conscious, environmentally friendly vegan. I've started a group here and we meet three times a week. There are only five of us, but we're passionate and committed. We are like-minded individuals, dedicated to fostering socially conscious, environmentally friendly life habits.

As president, and founder, of Murderers for the Ethical Treatment of Animals (META) I'd like to welcome you.

CHRIS COOK

Esthergen

"Your hormones," Esther's husband yelled,
"they're up and down, I swear!
And by the way, when's dinner?" Esther
said, "I'll be right there."

She sneaked behind him, cleaver raised
above his balding pate,
then started madly hacking, saying,
"Dinner might be late.

"In fact, I don't know what to make—
feel free to share your thoughts."
And on she slaughtered, diced, and cubed;
she cleaved his liver spots.

She said, "Why, that's a *fine* suggestion,
dear—I'll grill some liver!"
Esther's husband's body gave
a quick post-mortem shiver.

Before she finished up the deed,
she kicked him in the nuts,
and smiled a perky smile at his
eviscerated guts.

She stuffed his parts in Ziploc bags
to help contain the mess,
and shipped him off in little boxes
(no return address).

So now her husband doesn't bother
Esther anymore,
and Esther's feeling ever so
much better than before.

ANN M. COLFORD

The Girl Who Knew Magic

Once there was a girl who had magic in her heart. She knew she had magic before anyone told her. From her first blink of awareness, she simply knew.

Her name was Destiny, and she used her magic to create a beautiful cottage where she spent her days. She danced around the cottage and in the fields beyond. When she waved her arms in just the right way, fine gauzy silk wove itself into stunning outfits that she wrapped herself within. She wasn't lonely because six adorable winged kittens romped with her. If she and the kittens were hungry, she made cream pies as big as clouds appear out of nowhere, and they all ate their fill. Then the kittens licked their lips, washed their paws, folded their tiny wings, and fell asleep draped across her lap.

Destiny loved her magical world, and she never wanted to leave.

Her parents, however, did not believe in magic. When she danced and played with the winged kittens, her mother told her to stop leaping about before she got hurt. While twirling around to summon her silks, she knocked over a lamp, and her father yelled, calling her a bull in a china shop. She laughed at the vision of a bull in such a shop, but she knew from her father's face that he didn't see anything funny.

After a time, Destiny began to doubt her own magic. She stopped telling people about the cottage and the kittens. Soon, the kittens no longer came to play. At school, she wore the same outfits everyone else wore, because the other girls laughed at her when she danced to weave the magic silks. She felt unsure of everything.

Destiny grew and soon became a young woman. She barely recalled her days of magic, although sometimes she dreamed of a shimmering cottage with rooms hidden behind rooms and the flash of a wing in the tall grasses. The dreams unsettled her, and she wished for a way to block them out.

One day a young man came to court her, pleasing her parents greatly. He belonged to a respected family, one with no trace of magical thinking among their number. In his work, he commodified and incentivized and, eventually, monetized and multiplied, and this work brought him great treasure. He showered Destiny with gifts and much prestige. Everyone agreed that he was a marvelous match, and Destiny felt herself swept along with their convictions. The young man promised to banish all uncertainty from her world. His name was Security, and soon the two were wed.

All went well for a time. Destiny enjoyed her life of worldly abundance. One day while strolling in their luxuriant garden, she noticed a new wall along the back edge of the yard. Although she thought it odd, its appearance was quite lovely, and so she did not mention it. A few days later, another wall appeared along the front boundary of the yard, blocking the house from the road. But this wall, too, was remarkably beautiful, dripping with bougainvillea and filigree, and she rather liked the air of privacy that it lent. So she again said nothing.

When the third wall appeared, linking the first two and enclosing the garden on three sides, she felt a tiny flutter of concern. But Security had promised to keep her safe, and so she raised no alarm. She simply trimmed the vines and watered the flowers.

The fourth wall went up overnight, like the others, sealing the garden and the house within its perimeter. All distractions of the world beyond were held at bay. Even sounds respected the boundary. At first, Destiny reveled in the quiet perfection of her garden. No longer was her reverie shattered by the cries of children playing nearby. No more did the antics of the neighbor's dog make her pause and giggle, for she could not see the dog prance by.

Her husband continued to come and go through the heavy gate in the front wall, but Destiny discovered that she could not operate the gate's complicated latch. The walls kept danger outside, where it could not harm her, and for this she felt profound gratitude. And yet her restlessness grew. She yearned for newness. She yearned for uncertainty. Amid the perfection of her existence, she dreamed of chaos.

One day, Destiny summoned her courage and shared her feelings with her husband.

"But I've given you everything and more," said Security in a tone of indignation. "Your garden is a paradise. And the walls keep out all uncertainty, just as I promised."

"Yes, my darling, and I'm grateful for that," she replied. "But I miss the moments of serendipity beyond the walls."

"Serendipity is just another word for chance, my dear," he said, "and I promised to never take a chance when your happiness was at stake."

"But, oh, my happiness *is* at stake," she cried. "I miss the differences that each day used to bring."

"Ah, but difference is the enemy of perfection," he said as he stood to leave. "These feelings will pass. Always remember that I'm the one who supplies the magic for your perfect life."

After he left, Destiny wandered among the flowers. It was a perfect garden, to be sure. Her husband was right. And he had made it just for her. But nothing about it was magic.

She began to weep. In her despair, her heart cracked open, and the layers that had enclosed it for so long peeled away: layers built of fear, of the expectations of others, of shame, of the desire to be loved and to belong. When the protective layers had crumbled, all that was left was the tender beating heart of the girl she once had been, the girl who'd known magic, who'd taken magic into her own hands and made her own world.

Suddenly the air above her pulsed with the rush of wings, and she gasped. The winged kittens of her youth had grown into majestic feline angels, and they swarmed her, purring and murmuring with delight. Destiny giggled as she petted and skritched each magnificent cat in turn. The cats then gathered in close and, linking their paws, raised her up, up and out of the garden, over the tops of the beautiful walls, and high into the air. Together they soared above the village, past the office where Security earned his treasure, past the school where no one had understood her magic, and past the home where her parents lived out their monochrome days.

At the edge of the wild wood, the cats glided gently down into the yard of a humble cottage. It was not as grand as the home her husband created for her, nor did it sparkle like the magical cottage of her youth. It was far from perfect, and she knew her life here would hold great uncertainty. She would have to learn to live without the advantages bestowed upon her by Security. But she also knew that she was free of walls at last. With the magic alive in her unburdened heart, she turned to embrace the precious difference of this new day.

YVONNE HIGGINS LEACH

For the Greater Good

Our demon race comes from the ancient cradle
of the origin—the deep crevasses of the earth.
No human has ever seen where we thrive
among the depths of the lakes and seas.

Sadly our story goes:
our only Demon King with his single
gigantic leg and uncontrollable eye
began wiping out his own demon creatures.

For whenever his evil eye cast upon another
they were killed immediately.
So profound were his glances that soon
everywhere we tripped over our own dead kind.

Why I do not know but he could not keep
his one eye shut and so to find a proper solution
and to save our underworld,
I married him.

With a heart void of romantic love,
I do proclaim I am Cethlenn, the wife of Balor.
But do not pity me my sacrifice,
pity our King who I have struck blind.

ELISABETH SHARP MCKETTA

Your Beast

There are stories about
She who her father chased
Because her finger fit
A ring: stories too
Of the girl her father
Sold to a beast for a rose.
I tell them to my children
Though they don't like
Listening. They pat the dog,
Inquire about dinner.
I talk against their sleep.
I talk into the flames.
I talk boring holes into
Their sweet skulls.
They endure, barely.
In stories we blame the father
Because we don't want
To blame ourselves
For seeing the trick here,
The reason girls choose
The real estate of beasts
Rather than their home
Cottages: The Antagonist.
Anti-anything, otherwise
You're gone from the
Human race, you have

Nothing to offer, no square
Story to tell. Listen,
Children: each of these is
The story of the beast.
Your beast. The beast at home.
The beast who raised you.
The beast your gamble,
Even if it killed you.
The beast who ensured
With love that you would become
Something or someone,
Once upon a time.

LEYNA KROW

Sinkhole

The realtor showed us the house on West Garland Avenue and insisted it had everything we wanted.

"Look," he said, "there's a fireplace, granite countertops, crown molding, and a large sinkhole in the yard."

My husband, Alex, and I laughed because we thought he was kidding.

"No, really," the realtor said.

We told him we didn't want a sinkhole. That was not actually an item on our list. We agreed on this with absolute certainty. We always agreed with absolute certainty back then.

"I know," the realtor said. "But the house is a steal. Way bigger than anything else you'll find in your price range."

He was right. So we bought the house and put up a fence around the hole to keep the kids from falling in and for a while after that, we didn't pay much attention to it at all.

But then, one night a few weeks after the move, I asked Alex how deep he thought the sinkhole was. He said he had no idea. So, we went to look. We climbed our new fence and I held a flashlight while Alex leaned over the edge.

"I can't see the bottom," he said.

I stood beside him and peered in. It was almost as if the light was being swallowed up by the hole, eaten alive. We agreed it seemed sinister.

Then the beam of the flashlight began to fade and soon disappeared entirely.

"Piece of junk," I said. Overcome by a childish impulse, I pitched it into the hole.

"That's sort of wasteful, don't you think?" Alex said. "It probably just needed new batteries."

No, I said. I told him it felt good to throw the broken flashlight. The feeling alone was worth the waste. Alex chuckled at this. He always thought I was funny back then.

Inside the house, the flashlight was waiting for us. It was perched at the edge of the coffee table.

"What the fuck?" I whispered, not wanting to wake the kids.

"Seriously, what the fuck?" Alex whispered back.

I picked up the flashlight. I didn't know if I should be afraid or impressed. A minute earlier I had thrown it into a hole in our yard and now it was here, in the living room, on the coffee table. I turned it over in my hands to test its realness. I flicked the switch and the light came on.

"The sinkhole fixed it," I whispered.

"Wait," Alex said, and for a second I thought he was going to warn me to set the light down and back away – it could be dangerous. But he didn't. What he said was: "Let's try something else to be sure."

He found a picture frame that had cracked during the move. I waited in the living room while he took the frame outside. In a moment, it was back on the coffee table just where the flashlight had been, the glass looking clean and solid. Alex returned and we inspected the frame together. We agreed it was incredible.

After that, we used the sinkhole quite often. We dropped in scuffed sneakers, forks with bent tines, books with torn covers. They all appeared on the coffee table good as new. Soon, the sinkhole became just another feature of the house we were grateful for, like the dishwasher and the walk-in closets.

We never considered the effect the hole might have on anything living. Not until the morning our oldest son, Jake, woke me to announce in a tear-ragged voice that something was wrong with his turtle. He was holding the turtle, named Bert, in both hands. I could see the creature was sick. I didn't want to take both boy and turtle to the vet only to hear bad news. So, I led Jake to the yard and helped him over the fence to the hole.

"Put Bert in there and it will fix him," I said.

I thought Jake would protest, but worry for his pet had made him compliant. He set Bert into the hole and gasped when he disappeared. Back inside, he saw Bert on the coffee table right away and ran to him. The turtle was much improved. But a pale of concern remained on Jake's little face.

"Is my turtle a zombie now?" he asked.

"No, of course not," I told him. "Zombies are dead things that come back to life. Bert was just sick. The sinkhole made him better"

As soon as I said those words – *The sinkhole made him better* – I felt a kind shiver run through me. Like I'd just found the answer to a very important question I hadn't even thought to ask.

I began to wonder what the sinkhole could do to me, if I put myself in it.

I wasn't sick like Bert. I wasn't broken like our clock radio. But I wasn't the best version of me, either. I was thirty-eight and I had been hard on my body with childbearing, and before that with alcohol and hair dye and music that was too loud. The usual things. My character, I felt, had slipped too in my adulthood. I was impulsive and at times forgetful. No great crimes. But wouldn't my family be happier if I was improved? Wouldn't I be happier if I was improved?

I suggested this to Alex one night and he said no.

"I like you the way you are."

I thought he was just being kind. We were always kind to one another back then.

"But wouldn't you like me better if I was better?"

"No, because then you wouldn't be you."

I didn't see this as the compliment he intended. I felt he was saying my essential nature was a flawed one.

Alex looked into my eyes and I could see the worry creep across his face.

"Please promise me you won't get in that sinkhole," he said.

"Why not?" I asked.

"Because it's weird. It's a weird thing to do."

I promised, but I couldn't help but see this conversation as evidence for exactly why I needed so badly to go through the sinkhole: My logic was flawed, my thinking strange. What kind of woman wants to put herself in a hole? I felt strongly that if I used the hole to make myself better, I would be rid of such weirdness. I would no longer be the sort of person who wished to get into holes.

Alex kept looking at me but I didn't say anything because I didn't want to lie to him. We never lied back then.

I felt ready to get in the hole that night, but chose to wait. I wanted to be certain I was doing the right thing. So, for the next week,

I went about my life as my normal, flawed self. In my head, I kept a list of each mistake I made, every error a more perfect me would have been able to avoid – a burnt pan of lasagna, a forgotten birthday. And so on. Normally, I might have chastised myself for these missteps and later recounted them to Alex so he could reassure me they weren't really so bad. But instead I hoarded them almost gleefully. They were the evidence against myself. I was building my case for the sinkhole.

Then one night Jake went off for a sleepover and left me with instructions to feed Bert – what kind of veggies and how much. Of course I forgot. In the morning, the turtle gazed out at me from his cage with what I imagined to be a hunger-stricken look. *Never again*, I thought. I went straight for the hole. As I climbed the fence, I wondered about my entry. Should I dive? Cannonball? No. Such actions would suggest a kind of playfulness. But this was not play. It was work – the work of repairing myself. I stepped into the hole as if I were stepping off a curb. I felt myself tumble over once in the dark air then I was seated, legs crossed, back straight (no more slouching for me!) on the edge of the coffee table, feeling calm and perfect. Like I was someone else entirely. So, Alex had been right, of course. I was no longer myself. But the new and better me didn't care. The new me was content to sit at the edge of the table, waiting for Alex to come home so I could show him all the ways I'd changed.

HENRIETTA GOODMAN

I think they loved each other once, or thought

I think they loved each other once, or thought
they did, the day they fished Lake Elsinore
from a sailboat he'd bought—a whim before
they conceived me. But for years, when I thought
of them, I saw her as myself. She taught
me high waves, empty sky and distant shore,
his pride and disregard that grew the more
she panicked. I don't know whether they caught
any fish, whether he was competent
or reckless, savior or endangerer
or both, two men in one. He pulled the brim
of his hat down, opened a beer. It meant
that he had put her here and he could steer
or not steer. I was supposed to love him.

HENRIETTA GOODMAN

A booby trap:
my father was Bluebeard,

A booby trap: my father was Bluebeard,
though not a murderer. But how they killed
part of themselves to get away was still
a kind of violence. They disappeared,
his wives, but was this what he sought, or feared?
And who my mother turned into—the thrill
of his life spilling into hers—it filled
her, changed her, then she poured it out, the shared
undrinkable cocktail of their future
flushed. So, for all of us, a loss. She kept
a coat he gave her—the crushed velvet pelt
of fetal lamb, or lambs—patchwork suture
of black to white that loosened as it slept.
It would be mine, that coat, that shame I felt.

HENRIETTA GOODMAN

That garnet, that mistake— a kind of force

That garnet, that mistake—a kind of force
equal and opposite the one you made
before, a pool game's combo shot. You played
to test the laws of motion—less excuse
this time—you knew better, tried to seduce
yourself. His beauty helped, and so you weighed
the options, waited for your doubts to fade,
conceived his child, put on his ring. Of course
you were afraid of loneliness. You hung
new photos, labyrinth in every frame.
He looked like James Dean, shivered when you'd trace
the soft blade of his hipbone with your tongue.
And you thought that would be enough—the same
maze built too well again, the same walled place.

HENRIETTA GOODMAN

He showed me what he was— an altar boy,

He showed me what he was—an altar boy,
a drunk, a tragic hero, fingers stained
from nicotine. His posture—force restrained,
potential, not kinetic. He'd destroy
then resurrect himself, transformed by joy—
a passing radiance in darkness. Trained
to find the fatal flaw, I read his feigned
achievements, paralytic fear: alloy
of character and man. *Which way I fly
is Hell; myself am Hell*—Satan, my twelfth
grade English crush—and so I analyzed
the text and not the reader, not the why
of my pursuit of ruined beauty, wealth
of loss, not what, in me, he recognized.

KRIS DINNISON

Sea-Husband

My sea-husband asked me not to go. His brown eyes grew wide with worry each time I shed my skin to lie laughing and talking on the warm rocks with my sisters. As we stretched our naked bodies across the shoreline, the sun browning us until we were almost the color of the seal pelts we left hidden in the bushes, I felt the heat wake me up to a world of light and color unknown beneath the undulating waves. He kept watch as he bobbed off shore, marring the perfect freedom of our smooth skin, our long legs, our tresses lifting and dancing on the breeze as the water evaporated, returning to the sea. But even his vigilance couldn't take from me that moment when the last of the water left my skin and I was dry, completely and utterly dry. Not a trace of seawater or rainwater or any other kind of water on the whole surface of my body.

"Thank goodness," my fretful husband cried as my sisters and I retrieved our skins and slipped one by one back into the waves. I was the last to give up the land, and as I turned to cast one more look of longing over the sun-dried rocks, I caught a glimpse of movement. A figure, a man from the village, watching me. I'd seen him before in a small skiff, not fishing, just gazing at the waves, waiting. Even now, he didn't hide himself as the others had done over the years, men who had come to gawk and stare at our nakedness. This one stood boldly as I pulled and tugged my sealskin over the smoother skin of my naked body. His eyes were blue as the sea ice in winter, and his pale skin glowed against the dark cliffs. Something in me broke open. When I turned back to the sea, my husband was also watching me, but his eyes didn't hold worry this time. They contained something else, something less kind, but far more interesting.

After that day I returned to the rocks more often, and on my own. Sometimes the man was there. But even if I couldn't see him, I hid my seal pelt, tucking it furtively between two rocks near a sheltering evergreen. I would risk many things to be warm and dry on the shore, but not that.

Soon he became more daring. He stood closer. He strolled among the tide pools, searching for treasures. And one day, he spoke.

"I'm Fionn," he said. And the blue eyes that seemed so icy before crinkled and cracked into a smile.

"Hello, Fionn," I said.

"Do you have a name?" he asked.

"I do," I said. "But it's not something I just throw about for the wind and waves to take."

He shrugged. "Fair enough." He sat by me then, and we spent an afternoon talking of fish and weather and families who interfere. His wanted him to find a wife. Mine wanted me to whelp with the next season. Neither of us felt inclined to comply. When the sun dipped into the sky, I stood to go.

"Will you come again?" he asked, struggling to his feet.

"You know I will." I laughed at his question. Then I reached for his coat, running my fingers over the rough, worn fabric, the unfamiliar bumps and stitches that held it together. "Does it keep you dry?" I asked.

He nodded. "Does yours?"

I shivered, shook my head once, and then again to drive the drowsy, sun-made cobwebs from my brain. "You have to go."

"Can't I watch?"

I frowned. "Not this time." And I gave him a playful shove to soften it, but in my mind I was calculating the lateness of the hour, the time needed to return to the pod, to my sea-husband.

He finally left, trudging away over rock and sand, glancing over his shoulder at intervals, until he disappeared in the growing gloom. I raced to my hiding place and tugged and jerked at my pelt until it enveloped me. It felt tight and ill-fitting, snug in places that should have felt fluid. The pelt felt wrong, and I felt wrong in it. I swam away, and for the first time I felt an oddly-shaped hole under my ribs, a hole the sea couldn't fill.

I returned when I could, and stayed longer each time, stretching our dry days of conversation until my sea-husband began to question me. "Where do you go?" he asked again and again. And when I wouldn't answer he grew angry, then pleading, then finally whispered, "Be careful." His eyes stayed wide and brown, but they moved farther and farther away.

But I couldn't yet turn away from the shore, couldn't keep myself from that sensation of weight and stretch and ease that came from walking dry along the water without being in it.

The weather was turning, though. And I knew soon the coming rains would make the land as wet and cold and the sea. One day the sky was heavy with clouds, the sun barely generating enough light to warm me. I waited for hours before Fionn came walking from the village, his steps full of purpose.

"Will you stay with me?" he asked.

My eyebrows pushed together as the smile dropped from my face. "What are you asking?"

"I'm asking you to stay. As my wife." He stood far enough away that I couldn't reach for him, couldn't cajole him out of the dark mood he brought.

"I have a sea-husband," I said simply.

"And where is he now?"

I gestured toward the waves, turning to look as Fionn's eyes lifted to a point a short distance from shore. There, his head above the water, was my sea-husband, his brown eyes fierce, staring back at his rival.

"Where he should be," I said. "And where I should be as well." I turned toward my pelt's hiding place, revealing it to Fionn no longer a worry. I would not be returning, would no longer need to hide my treasure.

"It's not there," Fionn said, his voice sharp as the shards of rock that had cleaved off the cliffs and fallen in piles at the bottom.

I didn't stop, didn't at first understand what he was telling me.

"It's not there," he said again. "Your seal skin is safe, but it stays with me, as do you."

My feet faltered as his words sunk in, and a noise tore itself from my throat that was part scream, part seal bark, all pain. I heard my cry echoed as my sea-husband sounded his own grief and rage. I stared at him in the water, watching his struggle as Fionn came behind me with a dry, warm blanket to cover my nakedness for the walk back to the village. I stood as a stone, my eyes following my sea-husband as he swam back and forth, crazed with helplessness and fury until his brown eyes met mine one last time and he disappeared. Staring at the place he had been, the hole of longing under my ribs gaped and I was split in two.

The rains have come. I am never warm now. Never dry. I will bear Fionn's pup in the spring, a daughter if I'm not mistaken. And Fionn has me as his wife. So we have both done what our families asked of us, after a fashion. I return to the shore every day, scanning the water for my lost sea-husband. Sometimes he is there, but the distance is too great to close. I pine for the sea now as I once did for the shore, and I whisper to my future daughter of the dangers of monsters and men.

ELIZABETH KAYE COOK

When The Goat Gives Up Its Body, When The Body Is Consumed

I.

One-Eye and Three-Eyes despise their sister.
She looks so like other people, they say, and preen in their dressing gowns, coloring their lashes and warming their hands to the fire. By the time One-Eye and Three-Eyes powder their faces pale, Little Two-Eyes has already gone out with the bones of their meals.
Little Two-Eyes stands with the sheep and the goat in the grasses past the wood. She is to watch for wolves, but the staff shakes in her hand. She can bear her hunger no longer; she kneels and cries into the goat's white fur. The wet runs down its knobbed legs. Little Two-Eyes cries until her tears rise above the grass, and the sheep, bleating, begin to slip and float away.

II.

All animals are given the choice to speak at one moment in their life. Most stay mute, die silent. Yet as Little Two-Eyes's tears lift them up, and they float in her flooding, the goat whispers the words she needs to shake food from the air. The floodwater runs off.
Little Two-Eyes sings, and a jug appears, full of cream.

III.

Days pass. Little Two-Eyes starves for breakfast, gnaws bones at night.
She feasts with the sheep and the goat in the fields.
One morning Three-Eyes, tempting, leaves a single hard-boiled egg wobbling in her bowl.

Little Two-Eyes doesn't notice, is dreaming against the hearth as she laces her shoes. The egg stills, cools in its shell. One-Eye and Three-Eyes suck at their teeth, considering.

IV.

Little Two-Eyes still scrapes and bows. She thanks the sisters for their generosity, their crumbs, the burnt heel of their bread. But One-Eye and Three-Eyes sense a plump on their sister's bones. One day when Little Two-Eyes leads her goat and sheep to the fields, One-Eye and Three-Eyes sneak behind. They crouch and hiss as Little Two-Eyes sings. She sings until sweet bread and butter appear; steaming chocolate in a silver pitcher, broiled eel.

The goat hears them, sees them, tries to scrape warnings from its throat; its lips grow flecked with blood.

That night, One-Eye hands Little Two-Eyes the ax, sends her far into the dark for wood.

One-Eye slits the goat's belly, dragging the knife against the heft of skin and fat. Three-Eyes cracks the body into legs and loins, pours its blood in the dirt outside. Only the tongue sizzles in its skillet. The goat's notched eyes watch from their saucer on the stove.

V.

Three-Eyes says, We are sorry for our cruelty, for the years you lived so lean.

One-Eye says, Eat with us, this dish of meat.

Three servings on the table, and Little Two-Eyes cries happy rivers that pool in her dish. Little Two-Eyes saws off a strip of meat. Strange how the heart keeps beating.

The goat's eyes stare from their saucer.

The tongue in its skillet hisses and pops and tries to speak.

The three sisters chew with great concentration. The meat sticks to the roof of their mouths: thick, tasteless glue.

Little Two-Eyes scrunches her face shut and swallows. The goat's heart beats its way down her throat, and she sees then the tongue leaping in the skillet, those familiar golden eyes crying and bobbing in their saucer. Her hands fly up like birds about her face.

But you, little goat, wondrous creature!

You watch her flutter and choke. She spills your heart from its platter and soaks her shoes.

POLLY BUCKINGHAM

Clown Motel

When Bridget was allowed a weekend away from the home at Forest Grove, Chester brought her to the Clown Motel. It was Bridget's idea, though they'd both remarked more than once that it would be a creepy fun place to stay. "Just like old times," she'd said over the phone. "Just another Chess and Bridge adventure in Zanyland." Of course, it wasn't just like old times. It had been three years since they'd lived together; most of the time since then Bridget had spent institutionalized. He had his concerns: did she think they'd have sex? Did he want to have sex with her? With her newly sweaty splotchy face? He didn't think so, not with Duane so much at the forefront of his every thought, Duane's slow southern voice, like a man talking through a mouth of marbles, his long, slack face, the way half his mouth curved upward into a sly smile when he was thinking about sex.

Still, seeing Bridget was a great relief, and the laughter that erupted between them when they pulled up at The Clown Motel and saw that one of the clown's neon eyes had been shot out had been as welcome as a favorite pillow after a long cry. They had drinks in the bar, the walls lined with clown and midway paintings and a photograph of a woman with blue bunny ears, a big lavender bowtie, and a fuzzy blue bikini top. Chester had two gin and tonics. Bridget had six kiddy cocktails and told gruesome stories about the clientele in the institution—the woman who'd been abused by her teddy bears and had bruises on her thighs to show for it. "Them got some real claws," a guy with a permanently drunk expression told her when she hiked up her skirt to show him the marks. Or Raggedy Ann, as she called herself, who tied a tee shirt over her mouth like a gag waiting for her Andy. The sweat on the edges Bridget's face had shimmered in the dim bar.

Now they were in the room in the dark, both in the same big bed, and the TV was on. Bridget lay on her back with her mouth open snoring loudly. On the TV screen were two actors playing Chester and Duane. The actor who played Chester was Freddy the Clown, and the actor playing Duane was John Cheever. Freddy the Clown was a blue cloth clown with a checkered tunic and a solid blue triangle hat, the first toy Chester had formed an attachment to as a child. He'd also had an imaginary friend named Freddy, though he couldn't remember which came first.

"I'm sorry, Chester," John Cheever said to Freddy the Clown. "Things have just been so difficult at home."

"It's okay," Freddy the Clown said. What was the offense for which John Cheever was apologizing? Chester didn't know. He'd come en media res. Bridget pulled in a frighteningly long, loud snore. You'd think the kiddy cocktails would have kept her up. He should be the one sleeping.

"I married a monster," John Cheever said and put his head in Freddy the Clown's lap. His head smashed Freddy's small stuffed legs.

Freddy the Clown put his tiny cloth hand on John Cheever's head and stroked his silvery hair. "Your wife is not a monster, Duane," he said.

"You're too good to me, Chester," John Cheever said weeping.

Chester turned off the TV. He sat up against the bed board. He stared into the face of a clown on the wall. In the painting, the clown sat in a chair, leaning forward with his elbows on his knees. His expression was serious and a little mean. A car pulled into the motel parking lot. The lights shone onto the backside of the curtains. Car doors opened and closed eight or ten times. Chester got up and filled himself a glass of water from the sink. He'd only had two drinks, right? He sat up in bed drinking his water; the ac turned itself back on.

"Chester?" Bridget sat up beside him. "You okay?"

Chester couldn't speak.

"It's Duane, isn't it? I'm sorry. I should have asked you before. I just, I just thought you might want some time away from all that."

"He keeps complaining about his wife," Chester said and drank down some more water. It seemed to get stuck in his throat.

She wasn't going to say the things he didn't want anyone to say but that they said to him anyway: he's not leaving his wife, and what are you doing with that jerk? She rested her head against his shoulder. "Everybody wants you to be the sane one," she said. "Even him. It doesn't seem fair."

He reached over and touched her breast. She removed his hand. "I don't need that, Chester. I just need my friend."

"I'm sorry," he said as a wave dizziness passed over him and a few wayward tears moved down his face.

"Sweetie," she said, "can I get you a Xanax?"

He thought of his sister Margaret before her death showing him her medications. They were staying in a motel room together during a family reunion in Las Vegas. She'd held up a large Ziploc baggie full of bottles. "These are the psych meds," she said. "And these," she'd held up the second bag, "are the cancer drugs."

"An aspirin," he said wiping at the fugitive tears with the back of his hands. "I just need an aspirin."

ELISSA BALL

Service Provider

[S]eparate darknesses
mingle, then crawl to the common
dark, lost.

—Li-Young Lee, "Furious Versions"

I'll tongue kiss
your psychic wounds

well after midnight.
I'll make your darkness

throb 'til the
garbage truck comes.

Slowly,
    using circular motion,

I'll accept your streaks
of self-destruction and rub

my own bad-habit spit
into your lowered catcher's mitt.

Let's call our dual
whirlwinds   even.

Let's call each other's
scary parts

beautiful enough
to bathe in the light

of our lust—or whatever
it is we're calling this way

our bodies approve of each other—

harder and wetter
with each new worship.

I am at your service.
My knees scrape

the cold floors
of your inner abyss.

I'll lick
your smudges clean.

What's the worst nightmare
you can remember?

Should it recur, I'll
polish up my armor,

spit your demons
square in their round eyes,

and inform them
they may not fuck

with you tonight—because

tonight   you are mine.

ROB SCHLEGEL

In A Monstrance of Glass and Topaz

Nonny sits near the window

The first rogue wave

Shatters, ruining yesterday's

Mail. That's nothing,

She says, pointing to the horizon's

Black swell. Seconds later

I'm fetal on a bathmat, the house

Shaking inside a sound

Like a giant synth shitting

Metal Machine. An octopus

Erupts from the toilet.

Not my home, she says,

Ocean up and fucks us

Dandy shell emergencies

Love my body though

I'm through with Galene

Whom I never once betrayed.

Kelp trails a gull through a dead

Whale's ribs. Nonny paints

The kitchen melodramatic red

Till the octopus is a hologram

Traveling out the window

Through which I follow

If only for the sake of Nonny

And our desire to know

Each other and desert

Each other for new centers

Of meaning so that

The boundaries may reign

And in doing so be undone.

CEILAN HUNTER-GREEN

My Claws Ferocious, My Teeth Like Knives

I never meant them as riddles,
certainly. Maybe I have been alive for one hundred years.
Things like
scabbed rust on the thin parts of tractors
that makes me think of you.

I don't remember *you* at all.

All I did was ask questions
and kill and kill, sure.
I think this is how a god might feel.

Things like
hitting the mouth of an empty cup
things like
red berries against white

to you it's a riddle. The berries know what they mean.

No; I do remember
the cold blood thrill to swear you were mine,
hands laced around the heart.

SIMEON MILLS

The Idea

Lilac City Fairy Tales: Marry a Monster

SHANN RAY

For Jennifer
after William Blake

To see you walk in forested lands,
touch your face and never cower,
hold your hips in the palms of my hands,
the dayhouse in a flower.

SHANN RAY

Honeybush

When we meet
at the door,
over the counter,
on the table top,
against the wall
and backlit frontlit
pressed to the glass,
goodness
leaps up in us.

AMY RATTO PARKS

The Golden Mirror

I've always been unsure about the claim that emotional connection is a "basic human need," but I knew I wouldn't just happen to meet someone so I let my sister convince me to try online dating.

My online profile was honest, except for my actual name because I didn't want anyone Googling me. The site gave me a list of 10 women who might be "harmonious" matches, but I scratched most of them without much thought: no big smiles, no big eyes, and I hate bangs. That covered nearly the entire group, which tells me that the dating site's algorithm thought that my relatively dour outlook warranted some balancing by boobful, cardigan-wearing cheerleader types.

I did think one woman looked interesting. Her profile said she was a historian specializing in ancient Greek civilization. She liked to tour statue gardens and ride her Harley. Her photo looked professional because the light shined almost exclusively on her face, while her hair was shadowed. She was also looking away from the camera and I couldn't decide if I thought that was annoyingly performative or interesting. However, given that my own photo was taken of my good side, and that I, too, was looking away from the camera, I decided to think of it as interesting and sent her an email.

From that moment until now, everything has been a whirlwind. Our email exchanges quickly went from tentative questioning to feverish debate over foreign policy, the implications of teaching creationism in schools, and whether vegans are intelligent progressives or spoiled First-Worlders. We realized that we were pretty compatible, so we decided to talk on the phone and then we decided to meet. I had wondered how we were going to know each other in the crowded café, so she sent me a gift: a round, golden, palm-sized mirror with a snake engraved on the back. She said if I opened it and held it up to my face she would find me. All day before meeting her I carried the gold mirror in my pocket. I would pull it out, open it and close it. I knew I was already becoming attached to it and carried it with me everywhere. I decided that from then on, I would be the gold mirror girl instead of the girl with the terrible past.

I waited at a table in the middle of the cafe like she had asked me to. I opened the mirror and held it up and pretended to touch up my makeup, when I heard someone say quietly, "Don't turn around. It's me, but don't turn around. Look at me through your mirror." I tilted the mirror so that I could see her face and she smiled at me – not an eager, candy-store smile, but a wide smile that seemed to say, *Finally, here we are*. I smiled back and started to turn toward her, but her hands flew out to brace my shoulders. "I'm serious," she said. "Don't look at me." We talked that way for two hours. I felt electric being so close to her.

My sister asked if we're an item, which I guess we are since now we live in the same house. It all happened so quickly, but at our age you just know. I don't need flowers or chocolates to know that she loves me. I know by the way she sits behind me and reaches around to trace the scar on my face, calling it her "perfect little snake." I know by the way she strokes my hair with her fingers, braiding it into wide plaits. She says she's always dreamed of having hair like mine and I guess I can see why. She's quite shy about her hair and always wears a bandana or a thick knit cap. She won't let me touch it and laughingly says that it has a mind of its own.

We have had one argument. It was over the word "cursed." She kept trying to say that she was cursed, and I asked her if "cursed" might be too strong a word, since all of us have something we're ashamed of. She flew into a rage, saying that if I look at her everything will be over. I swear, her hair seemed to rise up and *move*. If I didn't know better, I would think it was actually alive.

Of course, things aren't perfect. She's quite demanding, but I follow the rules: never surprise her, ask permission before entering a room, always avert my eyes, and only look at her through the gold mirror. Sometimes I tire of it, but we all have our own little preferences, don't we? All relationships look strange from the outside, but this is love. I know in my bones that she would never, ever hurt me.

AUDREY DUFF OVERSTREET

Dances with Monsters

Date Night is our therapist's idea. She observes us bending over our cell phones in her office, scheduling it like a business meeting. We toss out and reject dates rapid-fire, struggling to find a night when my husband isn't traveling on business or we aren't required to attend one of our kids' extracurricular activities. We finally settle on a Tuesday evening, three weeks away. If our therapist knows we are doomed, she doesn't let on. She keeps her poker face in place as she bids us goodbye at the door and says, "Good luck." *Good luck?* It's like being wished good luck by your surgeon right before he puts you under.

We launch Date Night in promising fashion. Traffic is nonexistent and we arrive early enough to score a table near the fireplace with its glowing fake logs that never need tending. The waitress takes our wine orders right away. In the middle of the crisp, white tablecloth is a single votive candle, floating in a crystal bowl of water. I've learned over the years to nurse my dark thoughts in secret while projecting a jolly demeanor, so I gaze smilingly at the bobbing flame and wonder if it would be worse to die by drowning or by being burned at the stake. This is the kind of thought pattern my husband finds "depressing," so I ponder the question alone.

I allow the flame to mesmerize me, feeling myself glow with fresh lipstick and heavy eyeliner. I'm decent looking, with pale skin and long blonde hair I typically pull back into a low, messy bun. I never used to wear makeup, but my confidence has faltered in recent months as my battle to shed extra "baby weight" stretches into its third year. I am bewildered by my new fat-girl image. It's like I'm typecast as the chubby friend character, when what I really want is to play the lead.

Whenever I forbid my husband from posting a picture to Facebook due to a detectable double chin or a floppy upper arm, I pray Andy will say: "You're not fat." Instead he shrugs, irritated, and says, "You look fine." I wonder if Andy is angry that I've pulled the old switcheroo on him. *Now you see the pretty, thin wife, now you don't. TA-DAAAH!*

I decide it would be better to drown than to burn up. Less painful. When the glowing candle finally releases my gaze, I realize my husband is staring me at from across the mini flame-lit ocean between us. I'm almost startled, if not flattered. From the moment Andy sat down he has been riveted by the flat-screen TV over the bar broadcasting some sort of activity in which people interact with a ball. When I first met my husband, he told me he was a sports fan, but what he really meant was that he was like an alcoholic and televised sports was vodka. ESPN is as alluring to Andy as a singing siren to Odysseus. So when he graces me with eye contact at the Outback Steakhouse on our first date night in three months, and *not* during a commercial, I almost blush.

My husband is not a bad looking guy. His hair receded so quickly after the wedding ten years ago, he opted to shave it all off rather than deal with the friar look, and I respect him for that. His solid baldness works for his job as a corporate lawyer. He looks open and honest, like people used to think about cops before cell phone videos by Average Joe captured the overzealous beatings, tasings and shootings that have become as routine as the crimes police are supposed to prevent. I notice that Andy is grimacing at me with pain or concern, so I lean toward him and put my hand on his to encourage him to unburden himself. Maybe he's received bad news; has he gone to the doctor and been diagnosed with cancer? Was he denied a raise at work? Does he want to apologize for not taking me, and my painted lips, out more often?

He finally spits it out, albeit gently, like the delicate manner in which my grandfather used to pause mid-sentence to dribble his dip juice quietly into an old coffee can. "Hey, I know I've told you this before, but can you *not* run the dishwasher when it's half empty?"

"What the fuck did you just ask me!?" Whoa. This was out of character, even for me, to just whip out the f-word, first thing. It was like the book I recently read to my 5-year-old daughter, the one where a fairy cast a spell making one sister cough out diamonds and roses

whenever she spoke. I was apparently the bad sister, the one cursed to expectorate only snakes and toads with every syllable.

I cut my eyes to see if anyone heard and try to recover. "I mean, I'm sorry," I chuckle in a low voice, hoping I sound casual. "Are you concerned about the environment?"

"Here we go." My husband takes the opportunity of rolling his eyes to refocus on the game. I have been dismissed and he has moved on from this conversation, thank you very much, don't let the door hit you on the way out.

"Has this been bothering you a long time?" I press on. "Is that why you never do the dishes, because you don't want to waste water?"

"I can't tell you a *goddamned* thing without you attacking me." Andy sticks out his lower lip and begins stabbing at his cell phone with one finger. I imagine plucking the phone from his hands and dropping it into the candle bowl.

"The Dance," as our couples' therapist has dubbed it, now urges me to point out that it was *he*, not *I*, who attacked first by criticizing my chore abilities. To which Andy will be prompted to respond that his comment was not a criticism, merely a polite request… Then I would respond in turn…and on and on we would spin.

Instead, for the first time ever, I refuse to dance. I don't say anything at all. The television rolls on and the candle burns.

KATE PETERSON

Conceit

If estrangement is an ongoing death
with no resolution, then what is living
with a man who strangles you with his eyes?
Do you not die every morning when the clouds
glow grey? You hear glass break in the sink,
his morning mantra of blood and fists,
and all you want is coffee — pleasure you can count on.
The shrink says it's narcissism,
clinical, undeniable, and you should pack a bag,
bring the nest shaped chair if you must, but you must
run. You know this.

You see failure coming from a distance,
like the train that wakes you at 4:33 a.m., blowing its warnings,
but you won't let go. You lie in your bed and watch the ceiling tilt.
Remember when you used to count horses
instead of sheep? You knew what it was like back then, to fly.

You need to be the kind of woman you knew growing up
the kind who killed her own rooster with her bare hands
and ate him in small, thoughtful bites. And there he is again
with his disgust for your nostalgia. Your weakness.

Soon he will come back to bed smelling of rust
and apologies. He'll say the slate's wiped clean
and you should start again. Every night
you'll send a dove into the black sky.
And every morning, feathers
always feathers.

STEPHANIE OAKES

The Wild Wind's Girl

One moment, there was nothing. The next, there was a girl. She was only small in those days, a tiny bright curved thing in a bundle of swaddling blankets printed with appliqué clocks. She was placed in a field of wheat, when the moon above lit up the stalks like they were also made of light. The hand that placed her there wore a red leather glove, the kind that tears could skid off of when held to a crying eye. The person with the red leather gloves was upset, you see, to be leaving the baby in the field in such a way, but she had no choice. She had married a monster, and this baby didn't stand a chance growing up knowing she was half-human, half-monstrous. She needed to give the child up, and hope the wild would raise her.

And raise her it did. The wild has ways of fixing things that humans can't understand. But first, the child needed to survive her first night alone in the wheat field. A roving pack of sandy wolves snuffled the ground nearby and, beneath the earth, the mystical, rarely seen land worm was worming, smelling the scent of a child, something everyone knows land worms can never resist.

Just as the wolves almost converged on the place of tamped-down wheat where the baby lay, and as the land worm nearly broke the surface, its nostrils undulating at the smell of a baby, the child was discovered by a bear.

The bear hardly needs introduction in this part of the land. He is old as the fields, some say, and so massive he can often be spotted from miles away, trundling down hills and blocking out the sun. He is the height of a fully-grown oak tree. One single tooth could stretch the length of any of your feet, big toe to heel.

The bear rolled the child into his paws. The baby gazed into his huge brown eyes with her own considerably smaller brown eyes. In that moment, beneath the pale starlight, in the wheat-scented night, they belonged to each other.

And so the child grew, and learned the language of creeks, and grass snakes, and camas flowers, and bears. When she became sad and cried for no reason other than that she was a small thing in a wild world, the bear would fix her toast with honey, and not tell her that she was wrong to feel that way. The bear was gentle and good, and he raised her to be sad when she felt sad, but to be really happy when she felt that way, too.

The girl grew tall and broad, firm like the earth, until she was old enough to sense, even without having been told, that something monstrous lived inside of her.

"Who are the people who left me?" she asked the bear one day.

"There was a person, they say, who wore red leather gloves. They say she cried."

"She didn't want to leave me in the wheat that day," the girl said.

"Perhaps you are right," the bear said.

The girl wore the clock-printed cloth tied over her hair and, as much as she loved the bear, couldn't stop thinking on the people who had made her, who planted the monstrousness in her like seeds. She decided that it was necessary to leave.

The bear didn't understand. Parents rarely do, when their child tells them what darkness lives inside of their veins. The bear ducked his head, and said he hoped she wouldn't be gone long.

She walked far, surviving on flower bulbs and water out of deep streams, until she was in parts of the land that she didn't recognize, where the earth split into canyons and a great green river cut across the world.

There, she found a person with garments made of frayed navy cloth, small applique clocks covering the surface. The person was tinkering with something in a traveling caravan parked at the side of the dusty pathway. At the sound of her feet, the person looked up. Both sets of eyes widened.

"I—I know you," the person said.

"You left me in a wheat field," the girl replied.

The woman looked abashed. She crossed and re-crossed her gloveless hands. "I'm sorry," she said.

This seemed a strange thing to be told, after all this time. The girl felt the rumble of a roar percolating in her chest, and she didn't quite know why.

"I've come to learn the truth about myself," the girl said. "Will you tell me?"

"Well," the woman said. "Perhaps I shouldn't say. But it seems you already know. You are made of monstrous stuff."

"I knew it," the girl replied.

"But you are also half-human," the woman said, reaching out, but not taking the girl's hand. "That's something."

"What sort of monster am I?"

"There's only one kind," the woman said. Her eyes studied the girl's wide, sun-speckled face. "What will you do now? With this knowledge?"

The girl thought. "I suppose I will do something monstrous," she said, finally. "To see how it feels on me."

And the girl turned, and walked away from the canyon. She walked far, and every so often, placed her ear to the ground, knocking against it to listen for hollow places. At last, she located a tunnel, the size of her own waist, and crawled inside. She crawled for so long, and so far beneath the earth, her ears popped. There was nothing but darkness ahead of her.

At last, she fell through the roof of a dry, open den where the land worm lay curled in coils of cream-colored flesh. The worm's slits of eyes were two translucent folds of skin, shut.

Before she could reconsider her plan, the girl placed her hands around the land worm's neck and squeezed into its hot, undulating fat, but the worm was stronger than it appeared, and instantly its muscles contracted and it shook its head until the girl was flung aside.

"Why do you want to kill me?" the land worm asked.

"Because I'm a monster," she said, panting. "And that's the sort of thing monsters do."

"You're wrong," the land worm said. "Monsters don't kill other monsters. They kill the ones they love. Who do you love? Would you do that, just to prove this is you are now?"

The girl thought on the bear. She shook her head.

"Then perhaps you're not such a monster. Now leave here before I eat you up."

The girl scrambled out of the tunnel and ran through the night, back to the wheat field where a red-gloved hand placed her as a baby. Against the black backdrop of the sky, the bear's outline was visible on the horizon.

"So," the bear said. "Are you a monster after all?"

The girl nodded. "Yes," she said. "Though perhaps not a very good one."

"All right," the bear said. "Have some toast with honey now."

The girl found the bear's enormous paw, where her entire body had once fit, and followed him home.

HANNAH FAITH NOTESS

Whale Husband

Four o'clock: nobody came
to the wedding. Low tide,
on a beach pockmarked
with raindrops, the gnarled beds
of dead kelp buzzed with gnats.
I wore no shoes. My satin dress
shone slickly in what sun there was;
my updo slid and coiled around
my shoulders like an octopus
draped down my back.
My mouth pinched like anemones,
I watched. I waited. I plaited
seaweed, built a driftwood altar
lined with shells. Rain
stopped, hours passed,
the sun disintegrated into mist.
I refused to feel the cold.
The lapping water sluiced against
itself, and, all light gone, began
to glow. Far off, I saw him.
Spray of bioluminescent
light. He was far off from shore.

HANNAH FAITH NOTESS

Coop

We take the baby to a pale island
where almost nothing happens.
The whales have passed south,
and the sea currents weave
fog as usual. We forgot
the Moses basket, so the baby sleeps
swaddled on the floor, while you go
for a bicycle ride. I lie reading a mystery,
murder unearthed after years. The baby
twitches in his sleep. And the room
is an old chicken coop with an ugly
hand-lettered sign above the door. Sleep
when the baby sleeps. The hut begins
to turn on chicken legs. Baba Yaga,
the witch knucklebones. I don't need
the mystery — I know who did it.
I know. And the baby wails
for food and dozes off after.
Sleep when the baby sleeps. *It's not that*
I eat babies, says the witch, hovering
in mortar and pestle, *it's just that I need*
them for things. No, I say. *It's not*
that I'm eating you, says the baby,
it's just that I need need need.
I close the mystery and hold onto it
in the dark. Yes, I say. You come back
and open the hut door to daylight.
You tell me everything you've seen.

KAREN MUNRO

My Mummy

I came home early from school and found my husband Rich on the couch watching *The Wire*, wrapped head to toe in mummy bandages. He had a bowl of Smartfood on his belly and a glass of Stoup pale in his hand. He was trussed up like an undead sausage roll.

Seeing me, his eyes widened in the little bandage slit.

"Not all the time," he said. We sat side by side on the couch, the TV off, half the Stoup in me in one long gulp. Rich sat with his knees splayed, his hands hanging down between them. He looked like the kid at camp that gets bullied. "Just...more than I used to."

"I didn't even know you did."

"It just feels..."

I took his hands. The bandages were dry and cool, a little stiff.

"What I'm saying is," he said slowly, "that I feel an ancient and bottomless thirst for revenge against the men who invaded my tomb."

I hesitated. "Is this a sex thing?"

But he shook his head.

We went back to a woman we'd seen a few years ago. We sat on her flowered couch and she asked, "Are you still finding ways to date each other?"

Rich was wearing the bandages, but only under his clothes. He unbuttoned his shirt to show her.

"Okay," she said. "But when you put the bandages on, do you feel...powerful?"

Rich glanced at me. "I feel like stalking the English archaeologists who unwittingly woke me from my centuries-old slumber."

She squinted, as if trying to see Rich in a new light. "So...violence?"
I ground my toe into Rich's instep under the coffee table.

"No," he said. "No, no, no. You know, maybe it's a sex thing."

We sat in the Passat. "So, violence?" I asked. I tried to keep my voice steady.

Rich tugged at the bandages around his throat, under the collar of his shirt. He looked tired. "Not unless you're a nineteenth-century tomb raider."

"That's very specific," I said. "This is a very specific...thing."

Our therapist had mentioned fantasies and displacement. She'd given us pamphlets. Smiling couples at a dinner table, on a lawn, closing a bedroom door.

"Mummies don't exist," Rich said. "They're not real."

"They're real," I said. "They just don't usually wake up."

"I heard about the mummy thing," Rich's mother Louise told me. I could hear her plastic clip-on earring clacking against the phone. "Of course you realize it's not normal."

I was at school, watching my students file in. "Louise—"

"He never learned to throw a football, did you know that? And now this."

"Louise, I don't think—"

"We thought he was gay for the longest time. And I have to say." She lowered her voice. "He's never seemed exactly right to me."

I said, "Rich." Meaning: *Your son. Your son has never seemed right to you?*

"He needs an ultimatum. Tell him, if he doesn't cut it out you'll divorce him."

I thought of Rich asleep on the couch, his little pot belly wrapped in white linen.

"Tell him," Louise said, "that if he can't fly right, you'll find someone who can."

On the couch, our legs overlapping, the cat between us. Rich in his bandages, head to toe. Me in my Temple sweats. On the television, a mummy lurched around with two bullet holes in its torso. The music panicked.

"It's a love story," I said. "I mean, it's racist and appropriative. And sexist. But it's more a love story than anything else."

Rich, stroking the cat's little head, nodded.

Rich came out of his office and closed the door. There was something about the way he did it—quiet, final, pensive. By that time I was used to seeing him bandaged.

"What's wrong?" I asked.

He leaned against the kitchen table, where I was grading papers. "I had a web meeting."

"Okay."

"Video."

"Okay."

He plucked at the bandages on his cheek.

"Oh," I said. "Were you wearing—?"

"There were clients."

"Oh."

"Hassan called me back after."

"Okay."

He looked at the ceiling. "And fired me."

The cat, washing herself on the windowsill, paused.

After that, he was always bandaged. In his office, hunched over the computer. In the kitchen, frying ground turkey and egg noodles. On the couch, watching the same movies over and over. The old Karloff one from the thirties, the Hammer flick with Christopher Lee. The lesser progeny: *Mummy's Hand*, *Mummy's Ghost*. *Abbott and Costello Meet the Mummy*.

I came home late from a day of parent-teacher meetings and found him wrapped up asleep on the couch. I put away the groceries and poured a glass of wine. On the kitchen table lay his resume, marked up with red pen. He'd added a new bullet-point list of objectives.

- Come to life.
- Avenge wrongs.
- Date wife.

I took my wine back into the living room, where Boris Karloff waited on the screen. The cat blinked at me. I took the remote from Rich's hand and started the movie.

Vampires, werewolves, zombies—they all make friends. It's in their nature. The mummy, on the other hand, walks alone.

Maybe the mummy would rather not be there at all. Maybe he'd rather still be snug in his sarcophagus, instead of lurching through the storm.

After a while, you stop seeing the mummy as the bad guy. You start to see things his way.

After a while, you start rooting for him.

I took the bus to the fabric store, where I found a bolt of cream linen on the discount shelf. At the supermarket I bought a box of Lipton's, a couple of candles, and a styrofoam thing of beef liver.

In the kitchen, I set the bag on the island. In the living room, Rich was cross-legged on the floor, sorting resume pages with a mummy onscreen.

"Okay?" I asked.

He shrugged, and though I couldn't see his face I could read his rueful expression. "They need someone at Mattress Mart."

"I'll be busy a while," I said. He waved as I closed the door.

I made a strong pot of tea and started cutting the cloth.

The tea-stained bandages were clammy and at first they sagged. But when I was fully jacketed from feet to shoulders, I was warm. My body felt new, as if I'd just woken up for the first time.

I turned off the lights and lit the candles. I used the side of the toaster to pencil on a smoky eye.

Rich tapped on the door. "Can I come in?" I didn't answer. "I could use a cracker."

When the door opened I knelt on the island, holding the bloody beef liver in one hand. In the other, our biggest kitchen knife. Rich stopped short.

"My love." I raised the liver, ignoring the blood that ran down my wrist. "I give you the hearts of the infidels."

Rich swallowed, a dry click.

"Come." I waggled the meat. "Let their blood feed you. Let it slake your rage."

He staggered across the room and clambered up on the island beside me. With both hands, he reached for the meat.

"Taste," I crooned. "Taste, and be free."

He raised his mouth.

"But not really," I murmured. "It's raw beef."

"Yuck," he said, swerving away and burying his face instead in my bandage-wrapped bosom.

"My love," I whispered.

In the night-black kitchen window, I saw two bodies crouched on a blood-smeared dais. Their limbs wrapped in dirty bandages, their forms entwined. The candle flickered and they became a single monster.

SIOBHÁN SCARRY

Because You Said It Might Help to Keep a Dream Journal

First, a sororal death from ill-administered anesthesia. A camping trip in which the child unzips the blue tent and crawls away into the soft trees, never to return. On the third night, an actual collar and chain, and these words yelled to the cloudless sky: *I gave my whole body to this*. I slide each ready-made into the fear slots. My box of terror is true. The only surprise is the actual monster never appears. Fear unbundled from its source and free-floating. What strange fray, the mind no longer playing figure-ground, just letting its panic whip in the wind.

MARIANNE SALINA

Modern Monster Love

There was a time not so long ago when monsters believed in romance. A time when they understood what it meant to woo a would-be lover. My mother speaks fondly of her younger years in Paris, her early years of courtship with my father—young monsters in love as they were—and the pains he took to win her affection. He built intricate collages with waxy, blue-winged bugs and rare feathers foraged from remote forests. He sang ballads, read prose, shared cheese and wine, Bordeaux, Camembert, Flaubert.

But monsters today aren't so sweet. Romance is dead.

It was an early October evening that I walked along the Left Bank en route to meet my friend Sylvia. Halfway there, wistful and distracted as I often am walking the city streets, I suddenly stopped dead in my tracks. I locked eyes with a dark, handsomely complected man—a beautiful monster indeed.

He had a sparkle in his eye, a glint on his tooth, and his smile made all the blood rush fast through my veins. So clear and hallowed was this particular night, so quiet and still, that the moon seemed focused entirely on us. She extended one of her long, opalescent fingers, tracing a moonbeam around us, as though to say, "You two. Finally."

I drew closer. His expression changed. What seemed at first a moment full of promise had in mere seconds transformed. His eyes narrowed to devilish little slits, and his smile became mischievous, mocking. Then he raised his fingers in the air like a pair of bunny ears—a gesture I'd never before seen—and he bent them toward me, two pointers, up and down, up and down, like antennae.

He stared in a most lecherous way and bade me come closer, but I shook my head and backed away, confused and frightened. I ran the rest of the way through the streets, moonlight bouncing off sidewalks and storefront windows as I passed.

Sylvia understood immediately what had happened.

"Oh, they aren't bunny ears, love! He was flirting. That business with the fingers, it means *he wants to fang you*," she said, whispering the last few words.

"Fang me? No. Absolutely not."

"But of course," she said. "The way monsters do it."

I closed my eyes. "I don't want fangs," I said. "I want kisses. Whispers. Sweet nothings."

"Well sure, kissing is part of it," she said, "But so are teeth and nails and, depending on your flavor of monster, sometimes a little blood, too." She said this last bit with a sly grin, as though she knew even the first thing about kissing one of *those* kinds of monsters. She may have dated a monster or two in her twenty-three years, but not so many more than me, which was none. Zero.

"I get it," I said, "Fangs are sexy, but why the violence? Why not skip the biting bit and enjoy a little wine? Some light banter."

She shook her head and gently scoffed at this. "Oh, Gwyn. That's not how monsters do it anymore." She let out a long sigh.

Weeks passed and I woke one crisp morning to a dark sky pierced with tiny pockets of sunlight—luminescent white flags against a flat gray. I imagined this a sign of hope, and began my short bicycle ride to the library for a day of shelving and daydreaming.

As I rode along, I watched young children cling to their mothers before crossing streets, a tender, human gesture born of fear, so vulnerable mortals are to the crushing destruction of the world. "They are far too emotional and much too fragile," our parents would advise. "Their lives are too short. Never enough wine to ease their sadness as it goes by in a quick minute."

Monsters don't feel this anxiety. In fact, I've found an ease in my rituals and routines that I recognize as gentle and forgiving by comparison. Still, perhaps because of our excessive life expectancies, or because we can procreate forever, monsters, particularly monster men, have succumbed to a certain vulgarity that I can't explain or abide.

Morning eventually grew into longer shadows, and by late afternoon I'd worked myself into an even rosier mood, corralling stray
books and answering occasional queries, all of which left me feeling
useful. As I bent down to visit my favorite copy of *Alice in Wonderland*,
I noticed a monster at the end of the fiction stacks watching me in no
uncertain way. I stopped, clutching Carroll to my chest, and offered a
half-smile for the half-hearted hope I still harbored.

He was pleased at this, and for a moment he seemed to consid-
er exactly how to respond. Then, with a bit of hesitation, he slowly
raised two fingers to the air, flexed them, and smiled a wretched,
fangy smile. I dropped my beloved Carroll to the floor and ran to
the women's room for cover. When I returned a half hour later, he
was gone.

I rode home that night, my face buried in a wool scarf, and felt
deep to my core the particular exhaustion of defeat. When I reached
the Seine, draped in fog and distilled light, I stopped and leaned my
bike against the railing. I stared at the moon, big and full of swirling
shadows, and felt something inside of me crack open, an ache that
could not be contained. "I'm not of this world," I whispered.

I noticed then that I was not alone.

A man dressed in gray tweed stood nearby, his gaze fixed on the
moon, his bicycle also perched against the railing.

His pale, mortal nose was flocked with freckles and he wore a
pair of glasses, a bit too big for his face. He took his hands from his
coat pockets, cupped them, and blew against his fingers making a soft
cloud in the air.

When we locked eyes he gave a quick, nervous smile. He raised
one hand, and for a moment my heart filled with dread. But he merely
offered a little wave, as though tipping an invisible hat, and so re-
lieved, so happy was I to be the recipient of this tiny, human gesture,
that I let out a deep, hearty laugh, revealing all of my teeth and all of
my joy.

"Hi there," he said. "How are you?"

"Ah, hello! Beautiful moon, isn't it?"

"Oh yes," he nodded, his glasses bobbing up and down. "The
loveliest. A waxing gibbous."

"Yes," I said.

We stood like that for some minutes, staring back and forth between our moon and each other.

He told me his name was Eddy.

"My name is Gwyn," I said. And because it can be difficult to discern by moonlight, I told him frankly, "I'm a monster."

I waited for this to startle him, or for a panicked, hurried goodbye, but he nodded, an easy, knowing expression.

"I wondered," he said. "You have such kind, unburdened eyes."

I smiled again.

"You have lovely fangs, too," he said, sliding closer to me.

"Why thank you," I said, and paused. "But I don't bite."

"Neither do I," he said, and took my hand.

NICOLE SHEETS

Secret Convenient Bombshell:
A Found Romance

His eyes were so blue and so hard, they looked like chips of ice. She felt an unexpected surge of heat through her veins, a sizzle in her blood. The billionaire founder and CEO of Sud, named after the Slavic god of destiny and glory, one of the largest multinational corporations of sports apparel, equipment, accessories and services, seemed a mysterious figure in his black hat, a conjurer come to ply his trade with a magic wand, a mystic figure rising from the ashes of oblivion like a phoenix. He looked as comfortable in the saddle as she was in a desk chair. Animal and man moved as one. Were all horses that big?

Her face flushed with a memory of their furtive weeks of intense pre-Christmas passion. "Damn you, damn you for making me want you," she yelled. "Damn you," she whispered.

A memory of a three-carat ring stood firmly between them.

And she had only six months to make a baby.

His voice was deep and sexy. Never before had he found himself even remotely attracted to someone with multicolored hair and excessive piercings. But she was fascinating in an exotic-animal, priceless-piece-of-artwork way. Her skin was soft, surprisingly so for someone raised in northern Michigan, where the cold weather chapped skin raw. When her lips found his, she didn't taste like alcohol. She tasted like the spring breeze wafting over the prairie, fresh and sweet.

There was a wildness to him that intrigued her even as her mind whispered for caution. His past was a page that hadn't only been turned, but burned.

"You know your reputation," she said. "Scrapbooking does not make you a good role model."

A few wisps of fog floated through a field of bonnets.

"Scrapbooking?" he asked. "A man like me?" His jaw flexed, and he scrubbed a hand over his close-shorn hair.

She jerked free of his grip, her eyes wide with confusion.

"Scrapbooking has become an art form," he said, "with special papers and stickers and stamping." He resisted the urge to moan in pleasure.

Every word sank into her mind like a depth mine. She felt unwelcome tears start to prickle at her eyelids. She fought them, taking a deep breath through her nose.

He looked as if everything human about him had melted away. As if he was now a being of pure intellect and purpose, like a cyborg, an animate form of artificial intelligence.

Her retinas burned with the image of him.

"Damn you," she whispered. The breath left her body as she dropped him like a ten-ton millstone.

"Damn you," she yelled as she floored the gas pedal and aimed the car back toward Dallas.

Source texts:
Twin Heirs to His Throne by Olivia Gates
The Cowboy's Pride and Joy by Maureen Child
Secrets, Lies & Lullabies by Heidi Betts
The Billionaire Baby Bombshell by Paula Roe
His Baby Surprise by Lisa Childs
The Horseman's Convenient Wife by Mindy Neff
The Baby Surprise by Brenda Harlen
Her Rodeo Hero by Laura Marie Altom and Pamela Britton
Cowboy Daddy by Angel Smits
Honorable Intentions by Catherine Mann
His Secret Baby Surprise by Andrea Laurence

AMY SILBERNAGEL MCCAFFREE

Night

Snow started falling while we laid
on the couch, blue light of television on our faces

as if we were greenhouse-grown petals,
full like dahlias and no more fragile than boxed orchids.

Our eyes worked to memorize the flesh valleys
on the screen. I wanted bone and soft tissue,

wanted to find the membranes that revealed
how quietly snow slides across our branches and falls

to the ground. How sometimes the weight of it bends
the wood beyond return. I wanted hydration

and lipids, to see through your epidermal
masks and venture into our backcountry

of unmapped trails
towards trapped light

so that if I looked close enough
with my stronger left eye

I might see what sorrow burrows
through our veins.

AMY SILBERNAGEL MCCAFFREE

Marinara

honey, smack me into the kitchen next door and sit beside
    the white table
on the blue linoleum floor, cracked with coffee bean dust
    in the plastered borders

sweep lightly along the sink's faucet rim and let the tap water
    run over
last night's casserole dish so it steams the air with marinara again

and when you've done that
come to bed so quietly we dream only of garlic growing black fuzz
    in the dark cupboards
and me waiting for another Sunday afternoon with you

VANESSA LEA HALLS

Knights and Roses

Princess Ayla, with her soft brown skin and sharp brown eyes, was sixteen when her father made the arrangements. It was a common spell, the wizard had assured him, and very pragmatic. A princess locked in a tower cannot elope with a street rat, after all, nor be poisoned by a vengeful witch. Besides, dragons, the wizard promised, were reasonable creatures if you knew how to bargain with them, hardly dangerous at all.

Ayla disagreed. "Is this how you see me?" she demanded of the king. "A medal on a prize pig?"

Her question was answered the very next day, when she was carted off to a shabby fortress on the fringe of the kingdom with nothing but a scarlet dragon for company. In the five years since arriving at the fortress, there had yet to be a knight gallant enough to rival the dragon, though many had tried.

The years did, however, give Ayla ample time to get to know the dragon.

The princess was in the study when she heard the familiar clatter of claws on the tower's roof. She set aside her book, and pushed open the doors to her balcony.

"Here's one now," the dragon rumbled from its perch high above, regarding Ayla with opalescent eyes.

Ayla raised a hand to shield her own eyes from the sun. "Where?"

"Just there," the dragon said. To call its eyes hawk-like would be to grossly oversell the hawk. "Very fine equipment. Must be wealthy."

Ayla crinkled her nose.

"His horse is well cared for," the dragon added. "That's a good sign."

"A wealthy knight does not groom his own horse," Ayla reminded the dragon. "Wake me when his stable master arrives."

The dragon frowned. "At least allow him to proclaim his intentions."

"Oh, alright," the princess said. "I could use a laugh."

As the knight drew nearer, Ayla ducked below the parapet, just out of sight. The dragon spread its wings, ruby scales gleaming magnificent.

"Halt," the dragon boomed, its voice echoing across the desolate landscape like crashing thunder. "You approach mine own domain, where I guard jealously my treasures! Turn back, or taste my flame!"

"Taste my flame," Ayla said. "Does that fuel indigestion?"

The dragon smirked.

"It is I," the knight bellowed. "Sir Brynden of Blackrain! I have come to steal that treasure which is fairest, the hand of Princess Ayla!"

Ayla rolled her eyes. "He has never even *seen* my hands. He would be wiser to steal your golden chalices."

The dragon forced a straight face before speaking: "Enter my keep, if you dare, but know I shall not be bested."

"Foul beast!" Sir Brynden roared, drawing his sword. "I shall take your head along with your prize!"

"Leave the horse," Ayla called as the dragon took flight. "It really is lovely!"

That afternoon found Ayla mucking out the hen house. Years before, when it became clear Ayla's wait would be a long one, the dragon had stolen chickens and crops from neighboring villagers so Ayla could provide for herself. The garden began humbly, with cabbages and carrots, but grew with every gift from the dragon—shrubs, a hive for honey, and all of Ayla's favorite flowers. It even brought new books when Ayla had exhausted her limited library, which she would sometimes read aloud to the dragon on sunny days. Now the courtyard was all overgrown, a tangled little jungle. Ayla liked it that way. The lilacs were in full bloom, filling the air with sweetness, with the droning bees and clucking chickens adding their music. At times, she forgot the fortress walls, here in her wild place.

Beating wings signaled the dragon's return. Ayla wiped the sweat from her forehead as it touched down, careful not to disturb any of Ayla's plants beneath its talons. It carried a bundle in one clawed hand.

"How fares Sir Brynden?"

"He lives to fight again," the dragon said. "But he ran away so quickly he did not think to rescue his steed."

"You didn't!" Ayla gasped.

The dragon grinned. "I spoke to the horse. He knows his way home and was glad to be rid of the knight. He gratefully offered the contents of his saddlebags."

The princess laughed, accepting the pouch. Inside she found a wedge of cheese, a loaf of bread, and a shiny red apple—all rarities to her.

"A feast!" she said. "Thank you, and thanks to Sir Brynden's horse!"

The dragon nestled into the grass, and Ayla leaned back against it. Its scales were always warm as sun-baked stones.

The dragon said, "Surely, you grow weary of this place."

Ayla shrugged. "It's not so bad, thanks to you. Our lilacs are doing well."

"One day," the dragon mused, "we will find a knight worthy of you."

"Would you be rid of me so soon?" Ayla teased.

"I would offer you choices," the dragon said, a bitterness in its voice. "I would offer you freedom."

Ayla was shocked—she was jesting, but it made her think. "If only that freedom did not require the kiss of a knight."

"So many fates depend on a kiss," the dragon answered.

Ayla turned to the dragon, who avoided her gaze.

"I am forbidden to talk about the curse," it said.

Something took hold of the princess. She moved to the head of the dragon.

"My lady?" the dragon asked in alarm as Ayla took its snout in her hands. It watched in both fascination and horror as Ayla leaned forward to plant a soft kiss between the dragon's nostrils.

The world shifted. The hens screamed in terror as blinding light filled the courtyard, a sudden gale whipping up a flurry of feathers. Ayla shielded her eyes; when she looked again, the dragon was replaced by a knight unlike those she'd turned away—a knight in shining scarlet armor, a knight with a flowing mane of red hair and a smattering of freckles, a knight that opened her opalescent eyes and gaped at the princess.

"My lady," the knight gasped, her human body restored.

Ayla could not look away. "What is your name?" she whispered.

"Rose," the knight answered. "Rose of the Redwood."

"A true knight," Ayla said, taking Rose's hands in her own. "At last."

Rose shook her head and said, "N-no, my Princess... I am forever yours, but only as your monster."

"No," Ayla whispered. "You have always been my knight."

With their second kiss, Ayla's curse was broken, and a new kingdom was born.

Illustration by **MARCUS BROWN**

KEELY HONEYWELL

Jeannie and the Kappa
or Kappa Went A-Courtin'

Jeannie was the only child of a wealthy couple. They were dead-set on having both a girl and a boy, and tried to make it happen in the usual way. However, after a couple years of zilch, they got desperate. They tried a steady diet of rutabaga as prescribed by a book authored by a famous self-help witch. They sowed a carrot seed and made a wish over it, which had been recommended by a couple who swore it produced their orange-hued son. They paid a shaman a bag of silver on each visit to his hovel in the side of a hill. He told them they needed to visualize their future son with his guidance on a weekly basis. They stopped seeing him when he showed up late to a session driving a Tesla. After that, there was a deal with a squat man with long needle-like fingernails that fell through when the couple discovered that he intended to simply steal a baby.

While the couple tried everything to produce a son, they forgot they had a daughter to raise. Before they knew it, Jeannie had grown into a sixteen year old with a face full of acne and a voice as shrill as a banshee's when she argued with her parents. The first time they could remember disciplining her was after she had stolen another girl's magic nail polish and used it to paint her phone case to match her outfit. It was the first of many times she was caught stealing, and she soon acquired a reputation as a thief.

"Why would you take something without asking?" her parents asked her.

"Because I wanted to," Jeannie replied. "It's not like you guys ever buy me anything."

Eventually, Jeannie was deemed a lost cause and her parents decided it was time to marry her off. They held a pool party and told all the other couples they knew to bring their most eligible sons, and *no daughters*. Their Jeannie was to be the center of awkward teenaged attention.

During the party, her mother tried not-so-subtly to gauge her interest in each boy.

"Nathan's pretty cool, right?"

Jeannie frowned in disgust as the boy with a popped collar crammed a hot dog in his mouth.

"Hm. Well, he's interesting."

Jeannie looked at the boy her mother pointed out next. His skin was light green and the wide space between his thin upper lip and flat nose gave him a tortoise-like appearance. Atop his hairless head he wore a metal hat that kept a pool of water from spilling out of a round indentation in his skull.

"Looks like a kappa," said Jeannie's mother. "They say that can happen if you overwater your rutabagas."

"Ew, no. Gross."

From across the lawn, the kappa's big black eyes met Jeannie's and his eyeballs pulsed in their sockets as he grinned.

"Score!" Jeannie's mom said to herself.

"Oh, God, *Mom*, why'd you have to point at him?"

Her mother pretended to wave at a friend and walked away as the kappa approached Jeannie. His movements were as slow and smooth as a chameleon, no doubt in order to contain the water in his head.

"You're the most beautiful girl I've ever seen," he told her. "Could I take you out sometime? Maybe a walk through the park?"

Jeannie panicked. She tried to think of an excuse, or something to dissuade him. "If you bring me something... um, a silver bracelet, I'll go on a walk with you."

"Okay," said the kappa, nodding and smiling.

The next day he returned to the house and presented Jeannie with a bracelet of delicate strands of braided silver. Jeannie's eyes went wide at the sight of it. She repeatedly held up her wrist and admired it as she went on a walk with the kappa.

"I'd like to see you again. Could we have lunch?" asked the kappa on her front door step.

"If you bring me a gold pin, I'll have lunch with you," Jeannie replied.

What were the chances he could bring her a gift to top the first?

"Okay," said the kappa.

The next day he brought Jeannie a gold pin in the shape of a peacock with faceted aquamarine gems set in its tail. While they ate she watched the light bounce around in the green-blue crystals.

"I'd like to take you to dinner and a movie tomorrow," said the kappa as he brought her home.

"If you bring me a dress made of the feathers from every bird, I'll go to dinner and a movie with you."

"Okay," said the kappa.

The next day he brought Jeannie a dress so long it dragged on the ground behind her. The roc feathers around the neckline tickled her cheeks and made her laugh all night, much to the chagrin of the other people in the movie theater that night.

"I want to marry you, my darling," said the kappa after dinner.

"If you bring me a coat made of the skins from the most ferocious cats, I'll marry you."

"Okay," said the kappa.

The next day he gifted Jeannie with a silken fur coat that had a hood with the black face of a phantom moor cat. That night, Jeannie slept in the coat with the hood's feline face covering her own.

The wedding was arranged immediately. Jeannie was excited by the prospect of receiving more fantastic gifts from her soon-to-be husband, and she dreamed about what other wonders were in his possession.

When the wedding day came and Jeannie appeared for her walk down the aisle, the attendees were shocked to see her decked out in all the presents the kappa had given her. Unfortunately, it was because the items had been stolen from them.

"That's my dress!" cried a second-cousin.

"She's wearing my bracelet!" shrieked a teacher.

"And my pin!" yelled a friend of her mother.

"And that's my coat!" screamed an aunt.

"Thief!" they all cried.

Jeannie turned to the kappa. "You stole my presents?"

"I couldn't have gotten you all those lovely things by myself," he blubbered, shaking so hard some of the water sloshed out from under his metal hat. "I just wanted you to be my wife so badly."

Jeannie pointed at the kappa. "See? It was him!"

No one heard her. The crowd shouted for the return of the items and circled around Jeannie. The second-cousin from whom the dress had been stolen pounced on the girl and chaos erupted. The kappa was shoved away as the crowd constricted. Their hands pulled at the stolen items, catching bits of Jeannie's skin and hair. They tore at the girl until the dress, bracelet, coat, and pin were retrieved. By then, Jeannie was gone. They had ripped her apart until there was nothing left.

After the crowd dispersed, the kappa saw that his fiancée was no more. He promised himself that the next girl he courted would only receive a gift that he came by honestly, like a nice bouquet of mudwort.

SCOTT EUBANKS

In the Pines

Floyd lost his virginity at a Renaissance Faire. Separated from his friends, dressed as a knight, and drunk on hard lemonades, he rested on a log beyond the lantern glow of the tents. Through the slit visor in his closed helmet, he saw other revelers going between campfires, baristas and divorcees, clad in furs and implausible leather armor. At a noise, he turned.

Something moved in the purpling darkness beneath the ponderosas. At first he thought it was Bob Blass from the office trying to scare him again, but it was a woman. She stopped, stared for a long moment, a smile on her lips. Despite the dark, he could see her face as though it were lit from within by a candle: beautiful.

She strode toward him, barefoot on the pine needles—her black dress breaking character, but he didn't care. With each step she took, he was willing to give her more of himself. Until she stood before him, her charcoal eyes and lips the color of a freshly killed deer's liver were all he could comprehend. Before he knew what was happening, she pressed her lips to the visor. As he drunkenly tried to remove the helmet—there was a buckle somewhere—she had pushed him to the ground, her curled fingers clawing off pantaloons. She hiked up her dress to her hips, and he forgot about the helmet. When it was over, she kissed the cold metal and ran into the forest.

The following morning, as everyone loaded their cars and ate cold leftovers at picnic tables, Floyd kept finding excuses to look for her. Despite the hangover, he emptied water jugs and helped a group of barbarians load their Suburban.

He found her near the porta-potties, crouched on a stump like a gargoyle. Her dress wasn't black but a deep shade of green, the same color as her eyes. Her mouth hung open and tears that reeked of fresh pinesap streaked her face. She seemed sad.

Floyd offered her his hand and, after giving the grove a longing look, she took it. He told her his name. She sniffed his chest. When he opened up his Jeep, she climbed in, curled up on the back seat, and fell asleep. On the way back to West Central, he took the corners gently so as not to disturb her. She awoke as he unloaded camping gear. For the first time, she looked uncertain. He asked if she was hungry and managed to coax her into the house.

Inside, she went to the bathroom. Floyd, excited and embarrassed, scooped up laundry, video games, and a month's worth of takeout. He crammed dirty dishes into the dishwasher and oven. After a while, he knocked on the partly open bathroom door. She was standing in the toilet, pointing into the bowl with a frown. The water was gone.

To help her wash her feet off, he showed her how to use the bathtub. She startled him by lying down in the cold water. They shared a long look as the tub filled nearly to the edge, the folds of her dress wavering like seaweed. Her hair wasn't hair at all but fine, long feathers or leaves. Encouraged, Floyd leaned in to kiss her, but she slapped him so hard that he bit his tongue.

Retreating to the kitchen, he got a beer to cover up the taste of blood. On the news, he checked if anyone matching her description had escaped from Eastern State Hospital. What if she had mental problems? He thought: could he go to jail? Finished with his beer, he went to check on her and found her in the backyard staring at the moon, her feet planted in the lawn.

Turning off the stove light, he dragged the recliner into the kitchen and finished off two more beers. He drowsed as he watched her through the slider.

Sometime in the early morning, he woke to her straddling him. She lifted the back of his head and gently put the helmet on. He hadn't noticed it before but she smelled like fresh bark; her skin was as delicate and velvety as moss beneath his hands. As they made love, she whispered in a language like stones being rubbed together. Afterward, she fled to the bathtub where she had constructed a nest out of three half-dead spider plants, ash from the fireplace, and a couch cushion.

And it went like that for a while.

She would spend all day refilling the bathtub while he was at work. When he got home, he would watch her watch the moon until he passed out. In the small hours, he would awake to the helmet and the odor of pinesap. Her breath reminded him of the air from a cave—cold, wet, and mineral-laden.

A few weeks later, he had a few friends over to drink and talk about cinematography. Halfway through the first movie, Floyd noticed that Bob Blass was missing. He found Bob in the backyard squeezing her hip. Before Floyd could get across the lawn to hit him, she kissed Bob on the mouth. Bob screamed and unfolded into a ponderosa pine tree.

It was then that Floyd realized that she loved him, that she had been protecting him all along. He kissed her hand and she touched his neck. That morning, before she left the crook of his shoulder, he gave her his grandmother's ring, which she put in her mouth.

He dozed and when he awoke, she was gone. He found her in the yard next to Bob Blass, her trunk as big around as Floyd's arms.

He stopped inviting friends over after that.

The following spring, a little girl in a pale dress was at the back door. She had her mother's eyes and his mother's face. He let her in. She built a nest in the bathtub. Floyd showed her how to use the spout. From the kitchen, he listened to her refill the tub every hour as he eyed the trees in the yard and considered buying an axe. A couple weeks later, he bought the girl a portable DVD player for the tub, but she showed no interest. He did manage to get her to sit at the kitchen counter while he picked at his dinner, but she never did speak or answer to the name he had given her.

Loneliness had wormed a root into him. Most nights, he sat at the base of his wife's trunk wearing the helmet and recalling the percussive sound of her lips against the steel. By the fall, the girl had used up so much water that she was a teenager now, moodily standing in the backyard all night in a green dress. Her lips as red, waxen, and fatal as a toadstool.

When the girl began to disappear for longer periods, he knew it was only a matter of time. So one morning before sunrise in the backyard, he took the girl in his arms and whispered her name. Getting to his knees, Floyd asked his daughter for a kiss, the only thing she could ever give.

CLAIRE MCQUERRY

Snow, White Cake

I keep looping back to the start
like the gold that circles my finger now.
How I wish I could take the past apart
& remake it, but sometimes a seed

forces its roots so deep that you'd crumble
to clods of earth were you to tug them free.
Earthworms flopped & dried on cracked
cement when I met him. His smell was foreign

& familiar at once, his jacket black.
He lifted a single hair from my coat
& wove it into a binding spell,
a snare that drew closed slowly,

unbeknownst to me. I knew only that I wept
every day for a year, that a mound of stones
would bloom from my chest while I slept
& in the mornings I couldn't rise from bed. I had

visions. I was the fish whose gills flapped in air.
I was at the lip of madness. Madness
might have been a kinder end. The streets
flooded, awash with red silt. I knew then

he was a toxin in my blood, rendering me
lame—the poison & its antidote—even
at a distance, the tiniest flame
that wouldn't snuff. My life had once been

so orderly. Rocks were my garden's only
adornment. When neighbors came to the door,
anxious, with rakes, I saw it was fall: I'd been lonely
& had stayed indoors too long. *It's time*,

my monster said. I packed the car & drove
north to find him, following the signs:
a trail of blood & bones, a light snow.
The place names grew stranger as I neared.

Because I wanted to believe, I re-read his note,
that part where he'd written, *I'll make
you so happy*. The lies tasted sweet enough.
They dissolved on my tongue like white cake.

LAREIGN WARD

Mr. Medusa

My boyfriend refers to his not-quite-ex-wife as Medusa. The Medusa of Boise, to be precise, because he apparently needs to differentiate from all the other Medusas swarming the Western landscape.

"We're not in Boise anymore, Dorothy," I told him the first time he called her that, when he laughed at my jokes simply because I was the one telling them.

I've never been to Boise. I met Caleb here in Washington, six months after he caught her cheating again—it was the second or third time, depending on if you count that emotional affair with the barista—and filed the divorce papers.

On our second date, over Neapolitan pizza at a downtown gastropub, he told me that he had been married before, and, at least in the eyes of the state of Idaho, still was. Three kids. He admitted that he could have worked less and paid more attention to her, especially at the end. It might not have been enough, but he could have tried. He called her by her actual name, Eileen. Medusa came later.

Well, I thought, *at least he's being mature and respectful about this.*

That was a year ago. Nowadays, when he starts talking about her, the mental image I conjure up is of an actual monster. I've never seen her face, but I can imagine her, hair wild with serpents, mostly poisonous ones. Flashing green eyes. The look that paralyzes a man. I picture myself having drinks with this creature out of sheer curiosity. I'd want to know exactly how she became so hideous. Is it something you can feel coming on, or did she just wake up one day with a head full of snakes?

Last week, he texted me at work when I was in the middle of a meeting, something about how "she wants to ruin my life." I wasn't in the mood to hear it, so I wrote back, "Well, you did stick your dick in crazy," only it autocorrected to "You did stick your duck in crazy." He responded, "LOL," and with that, it became just a joke.

I have asked him plenty of questions, as he said he wants to be as honest as possible. I've asked if he planned to have kids with her (the first one was a surprise, but the twins were planned). I've asked why he married her in the first place (he loved her, and she needed health insurance).

They were together for nearly a decade. I tell him, and myself, that it took a long time for things to get so bad, and it will take a long time to untangle the knots.

"You just have to keep fighting, and the truth will win out eventually," I tell him. Without fail, he replies, "I know. But she's doing it on purpose." As if it would be somehow better if this was all some terrible misunderstanding.

"You are nothing like her," he tells me when we're cuddled in bed together. After that, he'll start listing the things he loves about me. My legs, which he loved ever since I wore those floral tights on our first date. My eyes, which he says are big and kind. My hair, which I started growing out after I moved up north. It's naturally brown, but I dyed it a bright auburn right before we met. The color fades fast, and I've been too tired lately to maintain it. He hasn't seemed to notice.

When he wants to, he can still make me laugh. The sex is still good, if less frequent. We'll cuddle for a bit afterward, and then he'll sleep, and I'll stay up for the chance to see him looking so peaceful. If I'm careful, I can touch his face and feel the stubble forming before he shaves it all off in the morning. He can't do facial hair anymore because she "liked it too much." Heaven forbid I should like the same things as her. If I do that, I might as well start digging through my hair with a fine-toothed comb for any signs of an impending snake infestation.

Of course, I've had my own bad breakups. I'm in my thirties now; the age itself comes with baggage. My last relationship was with a man who called me a sorceress the first time he couldn't get an erection. At first he said it jokingly, and so my apologies were also a joke as well. At some point, it stopped being funny. Our eventual breakup also happened in bed. He finally managed to get hard, and I started crying at the prospect of actually having sex with him again.

I cared, I really did. But I couldn't fix his issue, and when it finally fixed itself, I realized there were much bigger ones. I would have rather been the Maleficent of Boners than the person I actually became with him.

I used to think me and Caleb were in the home stretch, that once all this court stuff was settled, we could move on with our life together. I don't want kids of my own, but I pictured us getting a house together, one with a guest room or two for when the kids visit. Maybe we'd get a cat. Hell, maybe we'd get two cats.

But that was before Child Protective Services got involved, before she called them and suggested Caleb had been "inappropriate" with their daughter on his last visit. After she made that call, she texted him to say that, actually, he wouldn't be able to see Hannah and the twins that weekend after all.

So he hasn't seen them for almost three months. His lawyer doesn't think he should push for visits, at least not until the investigation is over.

Once, just once, I suggested to Caleb that being together might not be the best idea right now.

"Are you serious?" he asked.

"I don't know," I replied. We had this conversation two days after our anniversary, which was the same Friday he had a family court hearing in Boise. His car broke down on the way back, so I called the steakhouse to cancel our reservation. The hostess asked if I wanted to reschedule, and I forgot how to speak for a full minute before finally spitting out, "I'll call you back" and hanging up.

"Please be kidding," Caleb said. He looked desperate. I've never seen him cry, but his eyes looked wet. "She wants nothing more than for me to be unhappy and alone forever. She's trying to curse me."

I don't respond well to talk of magical curses, so I dropped it and resigned myself to being the antidote to wickedness.

So now I know enough, finally, to stop asking questions. That's not my job here. No, my job is simply to stand by him, brittle and still, waiting for the creature to turn her gaze upon us once more.

JORDAN SMITH-ZODROW

Have/Hold

It is sickness.
It is health.
In death, will you part?

A thought presses hot in the brain
or buzzes in periphery or sits
poised to lunge in the throat.
Sometimes, graciously, it dies.
One life in nine.

Richer in gratitude,
poorer in comparison.
In envy, you forsake all others.

When a problem cozies in the sulci,
deep in the fissures, they say to approach it
as eating an elephant, one bite at a time.
What is this? Four days in,
dark to the throat and slick past the wrist.
The stench and fevers and no end, no end.

Even here, worse to worst,

it can find something
to cling to, to protect.
A dagger, gartered against the thigh,
an idea of the better.

Cherish this flickering thing.
Love it with your one mind.
Always receiving, relentlessly giving.
Suggesting the frailty of moments,
whispering abstractions of eternity,
married to a monster.

MATTHEW WEAVER

The Fishwife's Tale

"Arizona?" My husband stared at me with those fish eyes. "That's the desert. I can't live in the desert, Bernice!"

I couldn't take it.

"Tell me what else to do, Barry," I said. "The urinal factory needs porcelain workers, and it's not like I can go back to Dr. Fowler."

I was a damn good dental assistant. But my old boss banned us when our youngest, Kevin, bit his finger off during a free check-up. Turns out piranha teeth are a recessive trait. Who knew? So I worked at the cannery until they went bankrupt two months ago.

Barry looked down at the floor. "I'll get work," he said.

I clapped my hands. "Who's going to hire a creature from the black lagoon? And even if someone were desperate enough, what, really, could you do?"

Now he was sulking. "I have skills."

"Oh yeah, there's a real market for abducting women and dragging them back to the swamp."

"It's not a swamp."

But we both knew I was right. He'd tried pizza delivery, night security—never got past the first night. We'd had a good couple months when he got the Sea World gig, but then the orca controversy resurfaced and they let him go, fearing additional backlash.

He didn't look at me, just kept watching the local news. Some soap opera actress was in town, plugging her new cosmetics line at the mall.

"If we went back—"

"Oh right. Madison is supposed to give up on law school to live in—"

"Don't say it."

"The wild." I leaned over, put my fingers behind his head, scratched his gills. "It's not perfect, but it's all we've got right now. And I think it's all we're going to get."

He sighed, slumped, his forehead damp against mine. If he were anyone else, he might have just finished running a marathon or been chilled from a fever. "Wish you'd married a vampire yet?"

I paused, just long enough to include him in the joke. "Or a mummy. Weren't you only buried in a pyramid if you were filthy rich?"

He kissed me. "I'm so glad I saw you on your honeymoon."

Then he went to the kitchen to grab another beer and scrounge for something worthwhile in the fridge.

He didn't, though. My first husband, Cole, and I were pulled over at some lovers' point because Cole didn't know how to change a flat tire. I was still in my wedding dress, rethinking the entire thing, when we heard a scream from the next car over, a red convertible.

I looked over and there was Barry, hauling some high school cheerleader over his shoulder while her boyfriend gave chase. He was intent on carrying her back to his mosquito-laden love nest. Of course, I didn't know about the mosquitoes then.

"Should we call the police?" Cole said.

I looked from poor momma's boy Cole to Barry. Shiny. Beautiful. Confident. Assertive.

"The cops won't come if it's not an abduction," I said, and before Cole could say anything more I was out of the car and running after him, yelling, "Hey! Leave her! Take me!"

Of course, Barry always rearranged the facts when people asked how we met.

And now Cole Wabash is assistant manager at three regional Waffle Huts. And I've got to pack up our family of six and move them to a job in the middle of nowhere or stay here and quickly get poorer. Can I pick 'em or can I pick 'em?

"Maybe we could do a long-distance thing," I suggested when we finally got into bed.

He said nothing.

"It's either that or risk you drying up," I said.

"That wouldn't happen in the lagoon."

"Please," I said. "It's bad enough at Christmas. And Barry Jr.'s skin will never allow it."

"So we can't go back, I can't go there and we can't stay here," he said.

"Pretty much. Sucks all around, doesn't it?"

"I bet you wish I never—"

I grabbed his face with one hand and pulled him in so close our lips were almost touching.

"Now listen, damn it—if anything, I dragged you into this. So enough of this pity party bullshit, it's not helping anything. I don't know what's going to happen tomorrow, but I know one thing—we're in this together." I kissed him and rolled over, blinking back tears, both furious at him and proud of myself.

He didn't say anything, just lay there. I could hear each time his gills opened when he exhaled. After a while, he got up and went down to sleep in the steam room.

In the morning, Madison needed gas money, the twins were fighting, I burned the Cream of Wheat trying to get Kevin to wear his clothes and Aubrey stopped fighting with Barry Jr. long enough to remember she needed to read five chapters of Moby Dick. So I think I can be forgiven for not noticing Barry wasn't there right off. I thought he was still pouting, to be honest.

I finally got the kids off to school and was looking online for discount plane tickets to Tucson when Barry finally came in through the front door.

"I swear to god, if you snuck out to buy one of your lattes," I said before turning to notice he had a large bundle over his shoulder. "You got a job at a laundry service?"

The bundle was squirming. Quite a lot. I gagged on burnt Cream of Wheat.

Barry undid the knot at the top and the bag opened to reveal someone I thought I recognized from "The Young and the Restless." Her makeup didn't look all that great as she looked from my husband to me, one of Aubrey's socks stuffed in her mouth, eyes terrified.

Barry looked up at me, his eyes shining.

"How much do you think they'll pay to get her back?" he asked.

JULIA ROX

Werewolf

Sometimes when I am alone I am convinced
I can feel my hairs growing. I do not know if
this is true, but I comb my hairs
for hours every night, keeping at peace
the army of living things growing out of
my body. Sometimes when I am alone I
think about how I am not really alone, how I can
hear the neighbors laughing, their
feet creaking across wooden floor boards,
handing someone a drink, taking dishes to
the kitchen. When they laugh, it fills my room
like ghosts, echoing through my baseboard heaters.
I sing to myself in the kitchen, hoping they hear
me as they stumble out into the night like moths.
They wonder about the strange music,
but no one asks out loud.

What is the lifespan of a moth? Silkworm moths
survive only a week after emerging from their
cocoons. What is the lifespan of one hair?
I collect handfuls from the shower drain
and leave them outside for the
birds to build nests with.
Sometimes I eat the birds. Sometimes
I eat the moths. I am feeding an army.
I watch them die— a lifespan stretched out
like a sentence, ending with an exclamation point.
I pick my teeth with their bones, and wonder
what is the lifespan of loneliness?
I do not ask out loud, but
it echoes through the house.

KARIN SCHALM

The Silver Swan

There once was a princess who had two older sisters, a queen for a mother and a king for a father. The royal family seemed happy, but they spent little time together because they were busy running a kingdom. When the princess came of age, she was granted three wishes like her sisters before her. The sisters had used their wishes wisely to create health and prosperity for all. The youngest princess was expected to do the same.

Pondering her wishes, the princess thought about the broken mill and how all the grain in the kingdom had to be ground by hand. Flour was not as light and fluffy as it once was. Breads were coarse; cakes rose only halfway. She could wish for the mill's repair but she did not.

A wild boar was sighted in the village close to the forest. The beast had scared children with its ugly, curved teeth and bristly snout. She could wish for its capture and release on the far side of the woods but she did not.

Most of all, without knowing it, the princess wished for love. Because she was young, she asked instead to be the richest and most beautiful person in all the land. As soon as she spoke her wishes, they became true.

The king and queen cried out in shame and turned away from their daughter, burying their faces in their hands. Her sisters cried real tears as servants stacked piles of gold from the treasury outside the youngest princess' quarters. Suitors arrived with the hopes of gaining an audience with this enchantingly beautiful girl.

Although the many suitors pursued her day and night, the princess remained unlucky in love. When she wanted to look for tulips in the garden, her suitors directed her to the archway of roses where they all proposed, one after another, only to be turned down. One day without thinking, the princess wished for a double to marry, someone to keep her perfect company. In the blink of an eye, her third wish was granted.

It was somewhat odd to have a double – "a me that is not me" – the princess would say. Within a few days, though, the two were inseparable. Touring the gardens arm in arm, they sought out the obscure dragon-tongued tulips. Eating their favorite foods together, they enjoyed the antics of court musicians and jugglers. Time passed quickly with much singing and laughter. Soon it was winter, and the cold drafts through the great hall caused them to call for wood in unison.

Trouble began with the birth of their daughter. The king and queen hosted a ball in celebration, but when the princess and her double tried to dance, they looked like they were stepping into a mirror. Colliding, they ended up in a pile of interlacing arms and legs. When the baby cried at night, they each got up to comfort her at the same time. Neither slept well. If the princess had a temper, her double had a temper to match it.

Annoyed, the princess wished for her double to disappear. She had used up all three wishes, so nothing happened. The princess tried putting red pepper in the soup because she hated spicy food and so did her double. Neither of them ate. She cut her long hair and gave her gold coins to the poor. Her double did the same. She decided to leave the castle, taking the baby to live in the forest. Her double went with them.

They walked for many miles on a rough trail, stepping on each other's heels all the way. Finally they found a lake nestled in the woods with a silver swan swimming on it. The lake seemed like a peaceful place, so they rested. When they woke up, the two of them talked for the first time in awhile. They decided to try and make a home on the edge of the water. Together they built a sturdy hut out of sticks and found moss to make soft beds for themselves and their daughter.

That first night they went to bed hungry but not unhappy. In the morning they gathered berries and fern tops for their breakfast. They set snares in the afternoon, catching a rabbit that they roasted over the fire with wild onions and mushrooms. They went to sleep full, completely satisfied with themselves.

Over time the princess and her double no longer looked or acted alike. One had curly hair and freckles while the other had straight hair and darker skin. One liked to skip along the trail by the lake while the other liked to run. They both enjoyed sitting quietly outside their home, watching the silver swan swim serenely across the lake. They fell deeply in love with each other as they took turns rocking and holding their growing daughter.

As the baby grew into a toddler, the seasons turned from summer to late fall. Food started to become scarce; the silver swan flew off in search of warmer lands.

The young family decided to head back to the castle before winter came. They dismantled the hut and made a bonfire from the sticks and moss, warming themselves from the embers of their home. Hiking back, they took turns carrying their smiling daughter. The three of them arrived at the front gates, pleasantly surprised to be welcomed by a very happy grandmother and grandfather and two laughing aunties. Everyone reached out for hugs, making a tight circle and taking turns standing in the middle of all that love.

KRISTINA PFLEEGOR

Spider Brides

The way I remember it,
the whole island burned,

sky orange with sugarcane,
ash piling in the corners of the living room.
Rats huddled in the ceiling,
centipedes fled into cool water pipes,
and moth after moth beat against
the window until
its wings gave out. Eyes
everywhere, small bodies fixed with shock.

In the murky after-burn
harvest machines with greasy arms
slid through blackened rows
to claw the crop from its skin.
Foreheads studded with lights,
they fed all night.

I tell you I can still see spiders
stream from those grinding throats
toward the field's edge
like charred hands drumming
their fingers on the earth top,
like ghost brides snatched
from half-spun lives.
Smoke veils trail from their shoulders;
they snag and shred on the rubble.

KRISTINA PFLEEGOR

Polyphemus Waits

But if you knew me well, you would regret your flight.
—*Polyphemus, in Ovid's* Metamorphoses

Halfway up the face of the cliff, a mouth of light. You might at first think you see a boulder inside, but watch it move an inch, as if settling against the cave wall. It grows hands. Its shadows twist into strands of hair and flatten into shoulders. It rises to put a kettle on the fire. On the hillside, sheep stir, and wind shoves loose grass into the ocean.

Come closer. Here is gentleness few recognize:

the way sky sits heavy over the shore, the way hands like ripped-up trees cradle what their lover left—the hard arc of nautilus, maybe bone, flecked with seafoam. Her kiss dried to salt on the fingertips. The creature waits and remembers.

His hunger is nearly human.

Notice how it has become his other half, a mountain rising around him. He stares like a lighthouse at the tide, which ebbs, and falters, and nearly returns.

KRISTINA PFLEEGOR

Not Even the Rocks

Inside the cave, I look out
a giant eye: framed landscape
of stepped basalt, sagebrush, bluestem,
faded greens and yellows of an old map.
All I hear are your footfalls on crumbled rock
and wind scraping the cliff face.

Bed down with me
on the rough floor
when the evening gets cool
and tell me a story,
one where floods carve canyons
and new rivers rage,
where history reshapes
everyplace but right here.

Keep me safe from the dark—
no, just try your best
to stay close
in this unfinished world.
Not even the rocks are safe.
As the sun snuffs out beyond the coulee
and coyotes bark and keen,
for as long as you can,
stay with me.

DARCY MCMURTERY

Crystal

True love broke up my marriage. Friends would later say, "You have a wife. What are you doing?"

I left those friends. What did they know about love?

They say that true love will break your heart. It also depletes you and leaves you penniless and cold. I didn't know that then. But I know it now.

I met her in the library. It was a rainy day, and I had been avoiding my growing inbox. I had watched the water run down the windows and briefly glanced up when a homeless man sat down across from me. He seemed harmless enough until he spoke to his demons.

"Only a trade," he hissed. I looked around for another library table.

He nodded at me and went back to his book. I returned to my own work.

"Just a taste. True love for your firstborn." I ignored him this time.

At some point I looked up again. The man was gone, but she was there. Shimmering. Promising. I couldn't shake the feeling that we were meant to be together. At first we'd meet a couple times a month. Then a little more. Always, it was the same thing: I'd wrestle with my emotions and soon she'd be there, ready to draw me into her embrace. I'd sail into calmer waters, free of my burdens. The visits were short and intense, but I knew I had to find a way to see her. She was a tease, that Crystal, and soon I was leaving work early to try to meet her before heading home to my wife.

Wives know things, and six months in she started to suspect something was wrong. There were many teary arguments and broken dishes.

She screamed words like *affair* and it turned me cold. I could never. I would never.

"How could you say that?" I shouted at the closed bedroom door.

There was no answer. I tossed and I turned that night, listening for movement in the bedroom. Finally I put my shoes on and headed out into the darkness. Crystal would understand.

I found her in a late night jazz club. I nearly swooned in her embrace, and we swayed together silently as blue notes bounced down my sleeve and into the dark club. I didn't go home then or the next night. By the third day, my wife called and sobbed into the phone.

"We can make this work. I forgive you. Let's try."

How could I say no? I stopped seeing Crystal. It was the right thing to do.

A year later my wife and I had a baby. She was beautiful. A raven haired, rosy cheeked beauty with large eyes and a quiet cry. Exactly what one dreams of when they think of their firstborn. We named her Hope.

I was content. I had the story book life: a beautiful wife, a decent home, and now a beautiful daughter. I thought of Crystal sometimes, late at night. It was natural, I told myself. It didn't mean anything.

Weeks of no sleep will weaken a man. I still thought of Crystal, only this time I reached out. We met again while I was at the park with my daughter. What had started out as a salve for my heart became an unbearable medicine. Crystal's claws raked through me, and I found myself making promises I couldn't keep.

Of course my wife found out.

There were threats. There were conversations. I couldn't tell where one began and the other one ended. There was even therapy. We had Hope and we had something worth fighting for.

I did what I could to erase Crystal from my mind. I started a new diet. I started running. Hope was my constant companion. I'd see mothers running through the park with their own babies in strollers. They accepted me into their group. I thought my wife would be jealous that I was welcomed into a group of shapely, sweaty mothers in lycra, but she smiled and shrugged it off.

"I trust you," she said as she tossed her gym bag into the car. Life was good again.

Until the next time. It was harder to meet up with Crystal now that I had Hope. I missed some work. Then I missed a little more. I sold a few things. Hope's godmother had given her a rattle. An ornate, silver rattle. I needed the money so I pawned it. It was a short term thing, I told myself. Next went my guitar, a laptop and the cuff-links I wore in my wedding. Gone. Then my job.

My storybook marriage ended when my wife came home to find me in Crystal's embrace.

"The baby is crying! What are you doing?"

I sat up in bed, disoriented, the taste of Crystal beginning to fade. How had I not heard my daughter cry?

"Get out," my wife shouted. "Go live with your monster."

The loudest sound in the world is a key turning in a lock behind you.

I turned my collar up against the wind and walked into the night.

Now I'm penniless and wander the streets looking for her, my one love. Sometimes I find her in the most unexpected places. Some nights I sleep without her, but it never lasts long; she always finds me. It's a marriage of pain and pleasure, of beauty and deformation, but I gave away my firstborn, my Hope.

DAVID ALASDAIR

Frankenstein's Green Card

"Prometheus," he says, leaning over the hostess. "Table for two."

"Yes, I have you," says the hostess, craning her neck. The creature in front of her is eight feet tall, dressed in an elegantly vintage black velvet sport coat, over which falls lustrous, flowing black hair, and a pair of black-framed Burberry eyeglasses which disguise his dull, yellow eyes. "If you'd like to follow me," she says, and the creature motions for his dinner guest, a woman with fair hair and a gentle but sad demeanor, to go first.

"Isn't this wonderful?" he says when they are seated. The waitress arrives to take their drink orders, and the woman asks only for water.

"Really?" says the creature. "Well, I'd like a Corpse Reviver Number Two. I'm going to treat myself. And if you could see to a few extra Luxardo cherries I'd really appreciate it."

"Of course, I'll see what I can do," says the waitress.

"I know it's only Wednesday, but I'm feeling Friday," says the creature in mock apology.

"Don't be silly, you deserve it," says the woman.

"I do, don't I," the creature chuckles. "And so do you. I insist you try it. After all, it's Wednesday for you, too," and the creature laughs again.

He reads the menu, occasionally letting out little gasps of delight. "What are you thinking? I bet you're leaning towards the chicken," he says.

"You know me better than anyone."

"A French waiter once told me," and here the creature adopts a hammy French accent, "*never 'ave the chicken, you can 'ave chicken at 'ome.*"

"I was thinking we could share the trout bruschetta," says the woman.

"*Brooskettuh,*" the creature corrects. "What a divine thought!"

The waitress brings the drinks, the sight of which causes the creature to applaud with just the tips of his overlarge fingers.

"I think we're ready," he says, "we'll share the trout *brooskettuh,* aaaand," and he gestures with a huge open palm to his companion.

"I'll have the duck please."

"Oh you devil, I almost picked that myself. But now I'm torn." The creature turns to the waitress. "What would you recommend, the pork or the lamb?"

"They're both really good," says the waitress. "The pork is amazing, and the lamb is very good too, served with a delicious parsnip puree—"

"Stop!" says the creature, and rolls his eyes around under his overlarge brow. "You had me at parsnip puree! Lamb it is."

"Very good," says the waitress, "I'll have that right out."

The creature rips into the bread. "Still warm! Warm bread and warm company, what more could I ask for."

"We should be roommates," says the woman.

"Wouldn't that be lovely," says the creature, salting and peppering the olive oil dip. "Unfortunately my student visa will soon be running out. I'll have to return home, more's the pity."

"Yes. I've been wanting to talk to you about that. There are ways around the visa issue."

"Hm? Oh, this bread. Something about that first bite of warm bread at the end of a long day."

"We could get married."

The creature chokes for a moment on a piece of ciabatta.

"For the green card."

The creature punches his chest.

"Wow… that's very—did you say married? Yes? That's so…generous of you…. You're a real friend, you know that. Only you would think of such a thing. What a gesture. Wait. We should have a toast. To a long friendship."

They clink glasses, and the creature downs his cocktail.

"We're a good team," says the woman.

"Yes we are," agrees the creature, reaching for more bread. "You know what would go well with this? A nice Rioja."

"I think it would be great."

"You do? Shall we get a bottle? Do we dare?"

"I meant I think it would be great if we got married."

"Oh."

"We get along so well. You wouldn't have to leave when your visa runs out; you know you don't want to go back there. You could stay. You wouldn't have to work any more of those under-the-table landscaping jobs."

"What a delightful idea," says the creature, forcing a pearly white smile through thin black lips.

"We could spend holidays together, we could travel, we had such a great time when we went to Seattle last spring."

"I'm practically married," he says with quiet apology.

"Well, I mean…" the woman trails off.

"What?" says the creature, "go on, say it."

"Technically you don't have a bride. He hasn't even made her yet, and who's to say he ever will."

The creature doesn't answer. He picks up his empty cocktail glass and looks for the waitress.

"You could be American, not a Monster."

The glass slams down. "The irony!" says the creature.

"We don't have to have sex," says the woman, rushing her words now. "We'd just live together. You could see other people, I don't mind, couples do it all the time these days."

The creature flashes a smile at the other tables.

"I don't even know if you do have sex—"

"Hey!" says the creature in an urgent whisper. "All the equipment works! And for your information it's 'creature,' not 'monster!' It's 2015 already."

"I'm sorry."

The waitress arrives with their appetizer, and the creature unfurls his napkin as if pulling the curtains on a new scene.

"Look at this, fantastic." After the second bite his smile returns. "Oh, this is spectacular."

"I love you," says the woman.

The creature drops his fork and begins rubbing his overlarge temples with the fingers of one hand.

"I've loved you since—"

"I don't love you," says the creature loud enough that other conversations around the room suddenly falter. "Why would I love you? Look at you."

The woman's head drops.

"You want to marry me, that's your ambition?" says the creature, his pearly white teeth sneering now through thin black lips. "Let me tell you what I see when I look at you. Poverty. Poverty of ambition, of ideas, of fashion. For god's sake, where did you get that blouse, *Tarzhay*?"

She holds her hand over her mouth as if she's been slapped.

"I was," the creature makes air quotes with two fingers of each hand, "*born* with nothing. No money, no friends, no property. I've lived in hovels, survived on berries and nuts. And now you think I'd be happy to shack up in some graduate-student apartment with you? Watch Netflix every night, go to a farmers' market every weekend? No! I won't live like that."

The woman knuckles away a tear.

"I," says the creature pointing at himself hard in the chest, his papery skin contorting, "am beyond royalty. I am Adam! And you think I might sink so low as to marry someone like you?"

The waitress arrives with the entrees, and the creature tears into the lamb, eating greedily. The woman doesn't touch her food. "You're a monster," she whispers.

The creature meets her gaze. The angry wrinkles fade from his face. "Oh my darling," he says. "You have to try the parsnip."

ZAN AGZIGIAN

No Love Bed

Suppose I told you a deep dark secret
like those kept hidden even from ourselves.
Perhaps I never tell anything else.
Could you keep this one secret inside now?
I'll even trust you *before* I tell you,
not knowing you. For, once a secret, not
always a secret. Does that label me
a cheat to tell you like adultery
without the betrayal? We're only hitched
if we've been united in ritual.
Suppose marriage is a monster that lives
under my bed. I try to keep hidden
in dust, (but it tries to keep) with regret.
It never wrapped its sacred arms round me.

Been spared the vows, the first dances, have not
succumbed to walking an aisle in white.
It's about shame, halfway glued to the bed
by a haunting probe, unable to move,
yet arise, be awake here, now, world swoops
down like a cut, tries to kidnap the dance
of swan from black to white and back again.
It's sometimes bold enough to sit by me

when I am alone, so full of longing,
Other times, in the tub, waiting to drown
right then and there—out of vengeance for not
playing straight with it in life.
Marriage reminds me that hot heads are him,
that glowing tip of wick is love that caves.

#

Within candles, fire recollects man,
centuries of mornings with them, surviving
the surface. Sure, I can show the claw marks,
the terror tracks that cause scars, a refuge
after dark, convinced that wild and free
is if I lean over, look under there,
if I get to the top, that's called safe.
Fast arrows, bullets, poaching, even rape:
There have been nights when I've run through it all.
The deepest intentions bear no witness.
The earth underneath opens up, filling
with compost, grow new roots from the bottom
of the murk, on the back of a Loch Ness,
moving from point to point, surrender fast.

ZAN AGZIGIAN

Storming Through A Tripping House

I hear murder trickle,
at once a sudden drop,
along Highway 200,
I feel one angst, one mother,
intent on keeping bed
in this white-washed wooden house.

(There's worry in this place.)

Segments widen,
breath on this corner,
separate corner, shining monster,
is an old and haunted house
where they trip out.

Along stretched scars, tar-smeared city windows,
she meets her lover's eyes,
slanted feather.

I stand where hems shedded seams
of skyline scarlet on their faces.

As I spy, I see their line-kind glances,
trusting touches
curved stringy muscles

making a place for gentle to go
and be enslaved in.

She holds fuschia flowers in her hair,
forces his arms open from dusty, dry manner.
Her neck embraces games
of reserved and drugged intrusion.
I lean against the hard bark,
hands on a cold beer,
see cowboy coats hanging
in the haunted house's hall.

I cannot catch a seat up front,
but wish that they would have it.
(Once again that he would have her,
once again that she would have him, once
again....)

She, laced in beads,
on Spokane acid,
raindrops (or are they teardrops?)
catch the sun,
and soak through her desolate cotton.

I see with my blind heart what is for me to see,
and full of rivers like a gulley flood,
they become a part of me
STOPPED IN SOME INVISIBLE TRAFFIC.

From the other side,
she lets him go,
but still feels,
she thinks she has,
his motion.

The road that she sees right.
He digs for motion's memories
from park to drive. The Motion.

And I see his body going down on her.
It reminds me of the body when it becomes

city. The body, when it loses pretty
to cement. And only has three colors of
A traffic light left.

I can't tell the difference
between a hot, abusive fight,
or the setting sun as it covers trees.
These double signals have me.
The Motion.
Their Motion.
Freezes love.

He's off the road.
He's failed the test.
Lost his license, can't get it back.
His was not a license to drive.
Or a license to let live, live.

If only love was two heads hard,
it wouldn't fade from their front yard.

ZAN AGZIGIAN

Poena Damni
(The Pain of Loss)

I was an Irish flower lover, once,
like your Chinese lover flower,
from the same stamen of an odorless truth
if truth had a scent

I haven't ever miscarried before,
all that blood, so unpredictable, unnamed.

There was a thought-out red once,
in a pinch, squeezing hard
the hand of a nurse,
thoughts of breaking out,
not feeling human through:
unworthyweightsuckedout
this bodyclumsy stamen

Unwilling to be loved gave me
a stamen okay to be stung,
pollen-packed up,
fly back to secure
new terrain inside familiar hive
deposit new honey not me

Catapults of cramps diminish well-worn tracks
across Bronx sterile sheets—
a virginal mountain galaxy
of nothing in front of nothing
simple veil of Destiny

Told to linger here for minutes *See stars*
wish for conversation with just one
whether up there or in
a drugged out imagination
sacrificing Divinity
like a pioneer ripping up
the earth inside
forfeiting Preciousness: a garden's rhythm
prematurely plucked

I am witness to the poverty of my past,
standing in Browne's Spokane ripping open
mail from Missoula, unfolding
a freshly killed poem, reading the red out
of soft petal words, whispering lyrics
over my own breath,
my eyes gazing upon the inside of myself,
line by line, the gift too late it's gone

This comb has formed thick compartmental wax,
a chamber trembling between pelvis and hand
monstrous, devouring love—the feeling I wish
someone had risked just once
for a stamen like me

BETH COOLEY

Rules for Breaking

Up in the hills the trails narrow and peter out; the caves burrow way back into rock. This is where they live—the centaurs—without modern conveniences like good internet service or reliable cell phones, over two hundred of them split up into smaller herds. Or groups, Leda corrected herself as she took it all in. Groups. Her boyfriend, Donny, said "herds" was culturally insensitive. Donny said he felt free up in the hills, like he was a part of something bigger than himself. Which must be why he hadn't called in over a week, hadn't come home in months, not even to do his laundry. He was acting like a real ass, worrying those kind people who adopted him and ignoring Leda, even though she'd been so patient and let him do what he felt like he had to do. But living in a herd, or group or whatever, was not the way he was brought up. A cave was not his home.

It was time for him to decide. It was Leda or them. One or the other. Especially now that she was running the ranch on her own. Her parents had died so quickly, so close together that the sheriff wanted an autopsy, which Leda politely declined. Now that she was all alone, she needed Donny more than ever.

Rosa, the mare she was riding, stopped and her ears went back, but it was just a couple of little ones frisking down the path. When Leda waved, they turned and galloped off laughing, cute as puppies. But aren't all babies cute? Especially the odd ones? Leda smiled, and then she saw the mares. Girls, Donny would say, because they aren't animals. But these sure acted like it, circling Leda and Rosa, snickering and whinnying, like they'd never seen a woman on horseback before.

"Easy now." Leda patted Rosa's neck and looked them in the eyes. Their hair was long and loose, their faces like angels, and they had on the tackiest shirts and jackets ever, like some kitsch parody of Dressage wear. On purpose? Or were they really that clueless?

"I'm looking for Donny," Leda said. "And don't tell me he's not here." The circle closed tighter and Rosa pawed the ground like she wanted to cut and run.

"Go on home," one of the girls said. She was more than pretty, a long-legged bay with hair that curled down to her withers, and copper eyes. "He's not your kind."

"But he's mine, nonetheless."

"You can't own him. Not like you own her." She nodded at Rosa who snorted and looked away.

"He belongs to her, too," Leda said. If they couldn't figure out what she meant, that Rosa birthed Donny, then they were just plain dense. But the girls tossed their heads and snickered. And when Donny stepped out of a cave they turned in one motion, like a gathering wave, or a bunch of sheep, and loped off laughing.

"Why didn't you answer your phone?" Leda asked.

"Battery's dead."

"Don't lie to me."

Donny grinned. He pushed his shaggy hair out of his eyes, and then he followed Leda and Rosa down the mountain.

By the time they got to Leda's ranch, he was wishing he hadn't come. Leda saw it in the way he trotted ahead or hung back, heard it in the way he answered her questions with flat little words, asking none of his own.

But she kept her gloom to herself. She'd been afraid of this, and so when they got to the house she cut him a big slice of the apple pie she'd baked that very morning. Donny couldn't resist anything with apples.

"I guess I ought to go see my folks," he said, handing her the empty plate without a thank you.

"I need some help first," she said quickly. "In the barn. The loft ladder's got a loose rung."

On the way to the barn he stumbled, once then twice. The Xylazine she'd ground up with the cinnamon was working faster than she'd expected. She got him inside just before he keeled over. She hobbled his hind legs and put a pillow under his head. She hated to see him like that, but sometimes you just have to show them who's boss. He'd get used to it, after a while. That's how they were. It might take a few days, maybe a couple of weeks, but Leda had all the time in the world to break him, and now that her folks were gone, there was no one to say it was unnatural or not right. No one to ask what people would think. Or how she planned to keep him satisfied.

In a month or so she'd announce the engagement. The photograph for the newspaper would be a head shot of the two of them. Of course, they would have to adopt, but wasn't Donny himself adopted? No shame in that. Maybe they could round up those little ones Leda had waved to on the trail to the caves. Surely their mothers would be more than happy to have them raised in a civilized home with the chance of a good, moral education. Leda would have to home-school, of course, considering how people still felt about mixed marriages. It would break Leda's heart for her babies to feel different than normal folks, so she'd keep them home where they'd be safe. And maybe, if she and Donny could manage to corral two, a little boy and a little girl, they could start their own herd. Or group or whatever. By the time the little ones were four or five, they could be bred. It was only natural. And what was to stop them adopting more? Between round-ups and breeding, they could have dozens of children just like Donny. And *for* Donny. Because Donny cared about that stuff. Diversity and Centaur rights. Hybrid justice and what not.

But they would be Leda's, really. Because, first and forever, children belong to their mothers.

It took Leda a minute to climb out of her daydream and notice the pounding. How long had it been going on? At the front door? No, behind the house. Maybe Donny hammering that broken rung. But the broken rung was a lie.

Unable to move, she looked out the window and listened until the pounding became cracking and then a final crash as Donny kicked down the barn door and galloped across the back field like a drunken beast. Like the uncivilized, selfish, cheating monster he truly was. Running back to the caves and the mares, and breaking Leda's cramped little heart.

RACHEL TOOR

Richer than God

Look. You just have to love him more.

He's richer than God. There's something wrong with every man—you just have to love him enough to fix him.

Take him to a salon and they'll trim the fossilized food out of his beard and snip that long mane right into submission. Get him some product! And, I mean, sure, the, um, extracurricular facial hair is a little gross, not only the fuzzy ears and bushy nostrils but, ick, those long black strands growing out of the top of his nose. You can pluck him. Pluck him! And while you're at it, some of those pimples are so ripe, so full, they're begging to be popped. All you'd have to do is apply a little pressure on the sides. Get the right angle, press with your fingers and watch the stuff come shooting out, a stream of creamy pus.

The fact is, any guy who's lived on his own for that long is going to need a closet makeover. Throw it all out—don't even try to donate to Goodwill. Believe me, no one will want white sneakers or polyester Sansabelt pants. Take him shopping. Better yet, just take his credit card. I bet he has a black AmEx. Buy him non-embarrassing shoes and shirts that cover his belly without groaning, and while you're at it you could get yourself some nice things. A Prada bag! I've always wanted one. And Jimmy Choo shoes, or Manolos. And La Mer skin cream. You could have rich lady skin! Oh, how I want rich lady skin.

I know you don't like it when he says your feelings are wrong. He's a rationalist. Feelings don't make sense to him. Anyone who keeps saying he doesn't give a flying fuck what people think of him— that's a guy who cares a whole lot what people think of him. You can work with that. Make him worry. Keep him a little off balance.

Being that rich, he probably thinks he can do whatever he wants. I'm sure he doesn't mean to be rude. He may not realize when he's scratching his balls or burping. I bet you can find something nice hidden deep inside. Wouldn't it be special to be the only one who sees the good in him? It would be like knowing a secret.

Imagine being married to a man with a private jet. Mexico for dinner! A weekend in Paris! You could visit your family more often. Okay, right, he refuses to meet your family. Or your friends. Or to go out in public. You could stay at the best hotels in the world and order room service! Think of the little bottles of ketchup and jam. I love those little bottles.

Would it kill you to smile and nod and agree with him? So he rants. And he hates everyone. Who cares if he likes to list the Latin names of the insects he collects and describes the smells of his many different flavors of farts. Smile and nod and use the time to think about all the shoes you could buy! La Mer skin cream! Prada bags!

Sweetie, you're not getting any younger. There was nothing seriously wrong with the last guy, the one who gave you flowers all the time. So they were from his neighbor's garden. He would have eventually found a job, moved out of his parents' basement, started wearing pants, and learned how to drive. You need to be patient.

And the one before him, the one who wanted you to call him baby and put him in diapers and then pee on him. Everyone's a little weird about sex. He was a good guy, an elected official! You're too quick to judge.

And the one before him, the skinhead who changed his name to Tranquility and wanted to be called Tranq? He wrote you poems. Come on, spelling is overrated. It's just memorization. And it's hard to find words that rhyme. I'm sure he didn't really mean that your lady parts reminded him of communist China. And *your eyes* and *imminent demise* sound nice together. It wasn't a threat. I don't think it was a threat. His jealousy was flattering. It meant he cared. He kept the guns out of sight, right? If you'd waited until he finished his parole you could have traveled together.

This one. Don't let this one get away. You just have to love him more. Love him enough to fix him. What they say about it being as easy to marry a rich man as a poor one? That's wrong. It's a lot easier to marry a rich man.

RYAN SCARIANO

After Midnight

An ogre, cold and hungry,
rough and dirty, she chews tar
and belches smoke, sneers and spits
her benediction of woe; that is,
until I see her warm eyes shining
off the gleam in the snow
and catch her fair reflection shimmering
in the river's frozen mist.
She has slipped her cloak of sweet stillness
over my shoulders. Tonight
I will marry this city.

Scarlett Hood

The crisp, cream-colored envelope arrived bearing Scarlett Hood's name in sharp gray ink. Before she even opened it, the colors – Silver Gray & Ivory – heralded an outcome that was the stuff of most girls' dreams. She had entered the recruitment thicket not knowing her way and emerged holding an invitation to join a Top House.

Scarlett had chosen the U over State because her high school friends were going to State. Scarlett liked her old friends, but she was ready to explore a new path. Still, the notion of getting lost in a forest of strangers was a bit frightening. Scarlett's friend, Mika, advised that the easiest route through the wildwood of college was to go Greek, because, Mika said, "Dorms are where your fuckability goes to die." Scarlett had only recently added fucking to her list of extracurricular activities. She wasn't eager to give it up. She decided to rush.

Unlike Mika's mother, Scarlett's mom didn't organize coffees with alums who would write recommendations on her behalf. Scarlett's mom did, however, supply Scarlett with a rushee's trousseau. In an act of apathy-inspired genius (Scarlett's mom hated to shop), she asked a woman from her golf round robin to make Scarlett a brand new rush wardrobe.

The woman was a tailor with a thriving business creating custom dresses for girls on the pageant circuit. Her preternatural ability to balance the organza high wire between sweet and slutty had paid for her Lexus. In her workroom, she measured Scarlett and told her with a wink that her magic touch would make Scarlett's assets pop. And pop they did. The bodice on each of Scarlett's new dresses was an asthmatic's nightmare, earning Scarlett wolf whistles from the fraternity brothers who lurked on their lawns, eyeing the female prospects. Sorority sisters were equally impressed. When Scarlett entered her first rush party wearing a bubblegum-pink sailor dress with a low-cut neck and back slit, the sisters asked, Topshop? Kate Spade? and Scarlett answered, Custom, and they were all, Whoa, and Scarlett was invited to the next round of parties.

After opening their bids, Scarlett and her fellow pledges received matching Silver Gray & Ivory t-shirts; then they gathered before an imposing, antebellum-style house. Alpha Beta Phi's double-doors swung open. The pledges started up the brick pathway but the members, huddled inside, barked, "Little Sister bonding!" and slammed the giant doors shut.

A water balloon sailed over Scarlett's head, bursting on the pledge in front of her. Scarlett turned toward its source as another balloon exploded against her chest, drenching her. The brothers of Gamma house, the fraternity across the street, came running, armed with wobbly, pastel globules. One downward glance and Scarlett realized the Silver Gray & Ivory t-shirts became transparent when wet. Members leaned out second floor windows, howling, "Fight like Alpha Girls!"

The pledge next to Scarlett pulled at her shirt, crying, "My cupcakes, they're like, showing!"

Scarlett, ignoring the visibility of her own cupcakes, grabbed the girl's arm. They skirted the Gamma brother's south flank, crossed the street and commandeered a cart of blobby ammo. The brothers, dazed by the bounty of Silver Gray & Ivory nipples, failed to notice Scarlett's maneuver - though her fellow pledges did. A second group of Alphas moved north, stealing another cart, cutting Gamma supplies by two thirds. Within minutes, the brothers were beaten from behind their own front line. They retreated to their house and the comfort of a keg as the double-doors of Alpha Beta Phi opened again, welcoming the Alpha pledges home.

As they dressed for the Bid Night ceremony, pledges gathered around Scarlett, commending her clear thinking during the attack, marveling at her ability to strategize under pressure, offering to French braid her hair. Scarlett was quietly thrilled. She did not feel lost and alone in the wildwood. She was a valued member of the pack. She belonged. She slipped her Bid Night gown over her head - a sleeveless, backless dress as red as her name – ready to pledge herself to Alpha Beta Phi.

One by one, pledges entered the darkened living room. When it was her turn, Scarlett faced the Council: The President, flanked by Vice-Presidents of Scholarship, Membership, Finance and Social. Each wore Silver Gray robes and held lighted candles.

Scholarship approached Scarlett holding a silver pin shaped like a wolf's head.

"The Wolf," said the President, "represents Wisdom. Do you, Scarlett Hood, pledge to try your best academically?"

"Of course," Scarlett answered. "That's why we're here, right? School."

Scholarship whispered, "The correct response is, 'I do.'"

"Oh," Scarlett said. "I do."

Scholarship fixed the pin to Scarlett's dress. Membership stepped forward, giving Scarlett an unlit candle. The President said, "The Wolf represents Loyalty. Do you pledge to place Alpha Beta Phi above all else?"

Membership tipped her flame toward Scarlett's wick, but Scarlett asked, "Would you mind clarifying what you mean by 'above all else?'"

Membership whispered, "The correct response is, 'I do.'"

"Sure," Scarlett said, "but it's a broad statement, you know?"

"My candle is dripping on the carpet," Membership said.

"All right," said Scarlett. "I do."

Finance stepped forward, holding a silver goblet. The President said, "The Wolf seeks to Serve her Pack. Do you pledge to attend (or, in the event of absence pay fines as detailed in section 23.7 of Chapter By-Laws) all Alpha Beta Phi philanthropic events, including (but not limited to) our Beach Party for Breast Cancer, Luau for Literacy, Mardi Gras for Multiple Sclerosis, Tailgate for Human Trafficking and (our best-selling ticket among Top Tier fraternities) Couples Handcuffed Bowling for ALS?"

"Could you repeat that first part," Scarlett asked, "about the fines?"

"A technicality." Finance put the goblet to Scarlett's lips. "The response is, 'I do.'"

"Wait, I…" Scarlett gulped what tasted like Bacardi with a courtesy splash of Cherry Coke.

Social approached Scarlett. The President said, "The Wolf understands that a Leader looks like a Leader." Social gave Scarlett an Ivory card with the number 20 circled in Silver Gray ink and a line awaiting her signature at the bottom. "Do you pledge to maintain the standards of Alpha Beta Phi and keep your body mass index at twenty or below?"

"Are you calling me fat?" Scarlett asked. "My BMI is twenty-three – it's normal."

"'Normal' is not an Alpha Beta Phi value." Social's gaze fell to Scarlett's hips. "And by the way? What big thighs you have. Better get yourself a decent pair of Spanx."

Scarlett snuffed her candle and tore her signature card in half. "I'm out." She burst through the living room doors, past the waiting line of pledges.

Scholarship, Membership, Finance and Social followed, growling, "No one quits Alpha!" and "We're a Top House!"

Pledges whimpered as the President pounced. "Give me that pin!" She sank her manicured claws into Scarlett's dress, clutching and tearing it.

Scarlett ripped her red gown down its length and freed herself of it, leaving the President on the floor wrestling with the shredded silk. A hush fell over sisters and pledges. They stared at Scarlett, standing naked and un-Spanxed before them. Scarlett turned from the pack, threw open the doors and walked out, into the wildwood.

EMILY GWINN

Dark Country

Even Galatea, it's true,
below wild Etna,
wheeled her brine-wet horses,
Polyphemus, to your songs.
                - Sextus Propertius

The sun will soon cast
shadows on what isn't
there.
Morning will widen sheets
into sails, begging the ocean to split
tides into men.

Oh Gods,
those butchers of lambs
hollowed him
into blindness,
sliced his moon
from sky.

They cloaked me
forever in black robes,
bowed his eye
from flame to fist,
I will never forgive them,
undone
by the terrible truth –

my milk-born lover
became dark country.

Soon, he will come into our room tasting
of chestnuts,
of bone and the hard knuckle
of marriage.

I will still hunger
for him –
though twice
I have stood in the doorway,
struck speechless from the sight
of his face.

Nothing good
will ever come of this –
what you call spring,
I call dowry,
what you call black ice,
I call husband.

This was not my
decision –
I have been asked
very little.

No amount light
will ever be enough.

TERRY BAIN

Eliza

I put the envelope on the otherwise empty desk and sat down in one of the two chairs. Eliza stood behind me with one hand on my shoulder as if to reassure me of her presence. She could easily have taken the seat beside me, but she preferred to stand, and I'd given up asking her to sit.

Lewis was our man. We didn't know his real name or profession, but he was our man. He took the envelope from the desk and moved it into a drawer, replacing it with a small pine box. Beside the box he set a single, sterile lancet. He slid the box lid back and removed a tiny piece of rough paper on which was inscribed a single word in a language I could not read, then held the paper in the palm of his hand while I took the lancet and pricked my finger.

Lewis had explained that the *shem* was not actually necessary after the initial animation, but that some believed it kept a golem supple, more human, less likely to become violent. I believed it couldn't hurt.

A drop of blood appeared on my finger and Lewis came around the desk so I could touch the red liquid to the *shem*. He whispered a few words over the paper as it soaked up my blood. Each month I wondered if he spoke a real language or just made it up as he went. But so long as Eliza stayed healthy and loyal, I didn't care much about the ceremonial details.

Eliza knelt beside me and opened her mouth, and Lewis placed the bloodied paper on her tongue and she stood again. Her hand never moved from my shoulder during the entire procedure.

Patrick returned to his seat. I picked up the pine box, closed the lid and dropped it into my jacket pocket.

"Well," he said. "Any news? Injuries? Changes in demeanor?"

I never had anything to report. I was happy with Eliza. There had been no outbursts, no violence beyond the few cats she'd killed. She'd been angry before, to be sure, but because she never spoke aloud, I was the only one who knew there was any danger, and I could soothe her before anything bad happened. Even if I had something to report, I wouldn't report it.

"No," I said. She'd never actually hurt anyone, had she? Not recently. Not that I could remember.

Lewis seemed pleased with my answer. He smiled.

"I've been reading lately," I said, and now I was looking at the point on my finger where a small amount of blood had reappeared. I licked it away and it tasted faintly of Eliza, of metal or stone or earth. I said, "In the golem forums, you know, I hear… people are making their relationships more permanent."

This didn't come out exactly as I'd planned, but it seemed enough. I wished I could make myself easily understood as I did with Eliza.

Lewis sat back in his chair. "I'm sorry," he said. "I don't think I understand."

He doesn't understand? But he must.

He understands very well.

"You see…" *Be strong. Tell him what you want in no uncertain terms.* "It's just that I think it's more acceptable. In some parts of the world. Ukraine, maybe? I can't remember. I've heard of weddings."

He didn't move. He didn't speak. He kept the confused, confounded look on his face, as if I'd said something that stopped time.

Tell him. Say it.

"I want you to marry us. Eliza and me. I want her to be my wife."

Lewis leaned forward now. He tented his hands on his desk in an utterly cliché way. He pinched his face before speaking. "No," he said, and that was all. The moment he said the word I felt the pressure on my shoulder increase, as if Eliza and her hand had become heavier.

"But she's every bit as human to me as any woman."

He still looked at his hands. Still tented. *There is nothing in your hands.* He glanced at Eliza but then spoke to me. "She's not a woman. She's not human. I can't marry you to a golem. Even if I went through the motions, nobody would recognize your marriage. Nobody."

"I don't care about that," I said. "I just want to be bound to her. As bound as humanly… you know what I mean."

The weight on my shoulder continued to increase, to the point of pain, and I nearly shrugged her off but also knew better.

"There must be a way," I said.

"No," he said. "I can't marry the mud any more than I can marry the rain. I'm afraid I'll have to ask you to leave."

His canned answer angered me, heat rushing up across my chest, and I imagined myself hurting him, smashing in his head with my bare fists. And these could have been my thoughts, couldn't they? They should have been mine.

Eliza moved so fast. Inhuman, yes. She was straddling him, bludgeoning him with her fists, just as I had imagined myself bludgeoning him, his head battered as his body was pinned to the chair. Poor Lewis, he hadn't even had time to raise his own hands in defense.

It took me a few moments to recognize the seriousness of the situation, to splutter out the words "Eliza…no!"

She stopped immediately. She almost always did as I asked her to. I stood up and went to her and pulled her away from him. His head was bloody and appeared narrow, too narrow for a human head, lolling to one side as if barely attached to his rag of a body. Blood flowed freely all around him and onto the floor.

Eliza took my own head in her bloody hands, leaned forward and kissed me, her rough tongue in my mouth, the taste of tin and clay and paper, the *shem* still sitting there, making her supple and human and non-violent.

It will be okay.

We had what we came for, didn't we? "It will be okay."

We will go now.

"Go home?"

Yes home.

"But who will take care of all this?"

Take care of all what?

The blinds were halfway open. I hadn't noticed the blinds before. Had they always been there?

"I don't know," I said. "I don't remember."

Let's go home.

Outside. Overcast. Led by my hand. A winter day but not too cold. Rain seemed imminent, unavoidable.

Eliza's hand. So powerful yet so loving and careful. She would not crush my hand but would hold it so I wouldn't let go, our fingers intertwined. Her hand seemed darker than usual, as if stained with something. But even as I watched, the stain seemed to fade as it began to rain on us, heavily, torrential.

Are we married now?

"Are we?" I said, wondering. Were we not married before? "Yes," I said, remembering something. "Like the rain."

SHERI BOGGS

Number Four

There are worse things than entering history as an ugly woman. But at the age of twenty-four, I did not know this. All I knew, besides a handful of words in English, was that my fate rested entirely in your hands.

Your hands—giant and meaty, with glittering rings jammed onto your thick fingers. The jewels at least should have helped me identify you when we first met but I was unfamiliar with courtly love and wasn't expecting an ambush. Do you remember? I was journeying to marry you on Twelfth Night but you couldn't wait. You had to see your bride. It was New Year's Day and I was still half seasick from the trip when you came to me with your courtiers, all disguised as peasants.

"A token from His Majesty," you said, or some such nonsense. The whole pack of you smelled like drink and you held out a closed fist to me, as if concealing from a child some wondrous treat. Who was this man, I wondered. A stout, cask of a body on legs that limped. Breath like foul water and a visage that reminded me of nothing so much as a pink, sweating ham. It was in the middle of such thoughts that you decided to kiss me, an arm slipping confidently around my waist as you tugged me to your looming bulk. Is it any wonder I pushed you away, swearing in my native German? I was a king's intended bride, not a sweetmeat for strangers. There were titters of amusement from your companions and as I looked from them to you, your face now a mask of forced courteousness, and I realized my mistake. I had rebuffed the King, who had expected to be recognized. You smiled widely, spreading your arms in a gesture of goodwill, and I saw a glimpse of the Good King Hal you must once have been. But I saw as well the glint of angry disappointment in your eyes; I'd need to watch myself.

"I dislike her," you exclaimed, once you were out in the corridor and supposedly out of my hearing. I learned what you actually said much, much later as the servants never tired of repeating the story of our ill-fated meeting, even, sometimes, with me in the same room. "She resembles her portrait little, Cromwell. I see no beauty in her. How could I take such a woman as my queen? She did not know me. *She did not know me!*" I didn't understand many of the words but I understood I'd made a mistake as your voice rose in fury and accusation.

"You must please him," my brother, the duke, had warned me. The English portrait painter had come and gone and while I hadn't yet received an offer of marriage, we were all preparing ourselves. There were rumors about you, of course, how you'd cruelly divorced your first wife in order to be with the second, who you'd had beheaded in order to marry the third, who'd died right after giving birth to your son. My fear did not matter to my brother, who saw an advantageous alliance and wanted desperately for me to be the one to secure it. I did not know what I wanted. To do what was asked of me, and to do it well, perhaps? It wasn't enough, of course.

In spite of our unlucky first meeting, we married. You in massive, furred robes, me in so many layers of gilded finery I felt I'd become a fat, gold purse. There was dancing and feasting, and yet more dancing and feasting. You tried to engage me in conversation. Parlez-vous Francais, mon cheri? Could I play the lute? You tried mightily but I continued to disappoint. I knew two card games, six needlework stitches and seven placid expressions. As you drank flagon after flagon of wine, you started telling me wistful stories of that other Anne, the one who spoke French, played several different instruments, and who sparkled with wit and ambition.

I knew what was expected of me on our wedding night—my brother had made certain of that. But that didn't mean I was eager to do the things he instructed me to do with you. I lay there in stillness and panic as you huffed and pawed, delivering messy, foul-breathed kisses that suffocated me while your hands gripped my breasts as if weighing a cheese. *Night after night after night of this?* I silently whimpered, while you jabbed at my most delicate area to make certain of my maidenhead. I tried to be kind, to not show my discomfort, but the next morning I heard you tell your trusted advisor, "I disliked her before, I like her even less now. She cannot be a maid. Are you my court jester, to bring me this, Cromwell? This is beauty to you? I find no beauty in her. And she gives forth such evil smells."

Evil smells? That is too far, even for you. I think we both know from whence the evil smells originated. That pustulent wound in your own thick leg—an old jousting accident, as you explained. But I know now you were trying to figure out how to rid yourself of me. In the days that followed I wondered what my fate would be. You'd already employed divorce, execution, and childbirth. What else was left? You sent me away from the palace. You refused to grant me an audience, even when my brother's ambassador demanded it. Word spread of my great ugliness, so ghastly the king could not force himself to consummate the marriage.

It was almost a relief when your men came in the middle of the night, demanding that I agree to an annulment. So my fate was to be divorce. Although I did not love you, humiliation washed over me. I'd heard of good Queen Katherine and how she had been treated. I thought also of my brother and how angry he would be that I'd cost him his alliance. But mixed in with the fear was no small amount of something new and thrilling. I would be free.

Something that had taken months to prepare for came apart in days. I was to lose my title, but would get to keep my life. Your advisor, Cromwell, who'd arranged our marriage, was not so lucky. From the gossip of my ladies I learned you'd chosen the youngest and silliest of them to take my place. I knew from passing your various Venetian mirrors that I was not ugly and in time, I ceased to care. In fact, there was a secret pleasure to being cast off. No longer did I have to fear your temper, your fumbling advances. No longer was I highly desirable as a pawn in the games of men. I stayed in England and learned your language, which I now speak easily. These days, I walk the grounds of my two houses. I read. I play the lute and enjoy what snippets of gossip I hear from your court. I might even take a lover as I know from certain glances of my male servants not everyone finds me monstrous. To you I feel nothing but gratitude. Your rejection was my salvation.

BEN CARTWRIGHT

Married to the Sea

Stand stable here
And silent be,
That through the channels of the ear
May wander like a river
The swaying sound of the sea.
—"On This Island" by W.H. Auden

Alice spied the harpooner knitting tatting on the pier, biting his lip with concentration, darting a small shuttle forward and backward in his hands. He held lacework up to the sun, inspected delicate knots, the mermaid tattoos on his forearms rippling. She proposed a grog shop first, then an evening at the symphony, and much later, handing him a ring she'd made from silver coins her brother melted down at the foundry, matrimony.

On Pier 5 in front of a priest and shipmates, the harpooner warned Alice that he was married to the sea. He hoped she could see past it. He would be married to her too, and she was the only island in his heart, the only small patch of green in a flat, dark blue, but they would need to start running. "Do you understand that the sea will want revenge?" the harpooner asked, face open and pale like the pages of a book.

"I do," Alice said. "I do, I do, I do."

Alice married a man who was married to the sea, so they hit the road. Inland, in a Cadillac as big as a whale, the harpooner turned pale and silent. A flat tire forced them onto the shoulder. Alice gripped the tire iron, and as she unthreaded the bolts, she heard him rummage in his duffel, produce his accordion, and squeeze out a mournful tune. She lugged the flat to the trunk, hoisted it in, and slammed the trunk shut. She looked out over the river gorge, the long bridge stretched across a thread of blue, the dusty earth in all directions. Her ears twitched, and with the strains of music she heard the susurration of waves. She breathed in and tasted salt in a place where salt had no business to be.

Alice and the harpooner parked on Riverside in a city far from the sea. They entered the lobby of a great and famous hotel, columns twisted like gilded bodies of snakes, a wide ceiling of glass that turned the lobby a milky blue. On an overstuffed divan, strains of violins echoing in the open space, the harpooner took Alice's hand.

"I imagine this is what it must be like," he said, peering upward at the glass, around him at the pale light, the musicians playing, "at the very bottom of the sea." Alice, feeling a sense of drowning, pointed to the bellhop with their luggage, and motioned toward the door. Further. They would need to go further inland.

Alice steered the Cadillac over collarbones of green hills, threaded their way south from the city far from the sea, and onto the Palouse. A storm rose behind them, great thunderheads like tufts of cotton. Pushed forward by a tailwind, the sedan creaked over ruts in the highway, rusty suspension making noises like the rigging of a ship. The sun sank, and a pale moon rose, white as bone. The harpooner did not speak. He did not play a note. They both understood the sea was following.

"It's getting worse," the harpooner said. The rain clattered its needles on the Cadillac's roof. Waves of water sluiced over the broken highway, and Alice's knuckles were white as she gripped the wheel. "We should stop. Stay at the hotel."

There's nothing out here," Alice told him. They rounded the curve, and he pointed upward to the butte where incandescent lights twinkled. He told her where to turn, what route they must take to coax the Cadillac all the way to the top, and into the parking lot.

Alice pulled the harpooner's heavy trunk behind her into the hotel. The desk clerk appeared when her husband rang the bell. There was some recognition in his eyes, Alice thought. She glanced around the much simpler lobby, walls of fresh-cut timber, coal in a Franklin stove glowing red in the corner.

"Things will seem better," the harpooner said, "in the morning." He marched ahead of her up the stairs, room key in his fist. Alice's throat tightened and her mouth felt dry. He had not asked the clerk for the room's number, or what floor it was on. She glanced behind her, but the clerk was gone. The rows of cubbies for the keys behind the desk seemed small and dark like open mouths.

"I'm going to need you to tie me to the beam," the harpooner said, handing her a thick coil of rope.

"Where did you get this?" Alice asked him. He did not answer her, his eyes cold and dark in the lantern light.

"She will try to take me tonight. When she does, I will not be myself."

"I don't understand," Alice said.

"The butte is high enough, it should be alright. We haven't much time."

Her husband made her put beeswax in her ears, so she would not hear him raving. Alice could not bear to look at him either, so she turned and stared out of the second story window. The butte was the highest point in all the rolling hills around them. The storm raged on, wind pushing through chinks in the walls. Thunder shook the panes of glass in the window. Each crack of lightning showed the surrounding farmlands, dotted now with standing pools like small mirrors.

Even with the beeswax in her ears, Alice could hear her husband screaming. She closed her eyes, but it didn't help. The lightning strikes were close, bright enough she might as well open them. She did, and looked out, and then she too began to scream.

The water rose over the Palouse. As she watched, it covered the fence posts. It covered the trees. The winding road that led to the butte was disappearing.

A rough hand gripped her shoulder, and spun her around. The desk clerk held an open straight razor, his shirtsleeves pushed up, tattoos visible. Behind him, her husband rubbed at his hands, free now from the coils of rope.

Alice jabbed the knitting needle she'd kept in her pocket since they'd arrived into the side of the clerk's throat. The man twitched, and then let go, dropping to the floor. She crouched over him, rummaged in his things.

"The sea wants to keep me," the harpooner said, looming over her. "I wouldn't sink. Blood is its only language."

Alice stood. She sliced her husband's throat with the open straight razor, its scrimshawed handle made from whalebone. She packed her things, and some of his. She willed herself to stay cold and hard like a piece of metal, the way her brother had taught her when they fought other children for food on the docks of the city by the sea. She kicked over the Franklin stove in the lobby, and made sure the flames caught the heavy curtains, and licked up the walls of varnished wood.

Alice drove east, crossing river after river, the Palouse, the West Fork, the Potlatch. Each time she came to a bridge, the sound of the water beneath made her look back over her shoulder. In Missoula she sold the rings, all she found in the Nantucket basket at the bottom of the harpooner's trunk, some of them silver, some gold, some with stones, some etched with names, far too many to count.

MEAGAN CIESLA

Whoever You Say You Are

On our way home from the Spic 'n Span we each had a metal cart with our clean clothes in it – mine were folded and separated by color and kind and Betsy's were heaped into a wrinkled lump of kaleidoscopic cotton. I was pushing my cart in front of me and Betsy was pulling hers. Before the engagement one of our agreements was that we'd always do our own laundry. I couldn't stand her crumpling my clothes and she thought I was too anal. We were just about to turn onto Main when I heard a low whistling sound and then a great *kahflop*. My cart shook so hard my hands flew off; when I looked down there was a 13" TV just fallen right out of the sky. It wasn't just a random TV – it was the TV I'd grown up with. I knew it because it was that same mustard color and my *Scooby Doo* sticker was still there with Scooby jumping into Shaggy's arms and the edge was peeling off at the top right-hand corner. And when I turned to tell Betsy about it things got really weird. See, Betsy's body was there but her head wasn't her head at all. Instead, it was *another TV*. Since she was pulling her cart and I was pushing mine her TV fell on her head instead of in her cart. I said, Betsy are you there? Is it you? And she took her fist and knocked the side of her television, which sounded like a tinny clank, as if to say, Yeah, Ray, it's me. Can we get this TV off my goddamned head?

So we tried that and we even called the fire department once we got back home and put our clothes away and I put my *Scooby Doo* TV in the closet, but the firemen who answered the call said there was no tool they knew of that could fix our problem. After they left I looked over at Betsy pouting on the couch with her arms crossed and heard a low mumbling. I thought she'd figured out how to talk through the screen but when I went to check it wasn't her talking at all but it was the TV that was on. The screen showed a baby in a crib staring up at a mobile with three canaries and a blue jay. I watched the baby watching the birds and then in the middle of eating dinner the TV shut off. I flipped the power switch back on but nothing happened; it had a mind of its own.

We lived like this for some time. Intermittently the television came on for brief bouts and then shut off again. I'd be washing the dishes in the kitchen and would hear something in the living room, the hallway. At first the TV showed the same baby doing boring baby things: learning to walk, babbling, stuffing Cheerios into her gummy mouth, but eventually one day the baby was a girl swirling a purple hula hoop around in her living room. It was hypnotizing watching it go round and round, so I was stuck on it for a while until the hoop dropped to the ground and caught on the girl's foot, which made her trip and fall into the coffee table face-first. There were speckles of blood on the beige carpet and when the girl stood up with a gash on her left eye I realized the girl on the television was actually Betsy, *my* Betsy, when she was a young. Betsy had a scar on the edge of her left eyebrow where hair would never grow and she filled it in each morning with eyebrow pencil; I'd thumbed that scar many times. When I realized it was her I turned to Betsy and said, It's you on the TV! and she put a palm on top of the TV where her forehead was supposed to be to say: You just realized this?

After that I couldn't stop watching Betsy's head. Even if the television was off I'd look through the glass as if staring longingly would turn it on again. I woke in the middle of the night once to Betsy's head showing her piano recital. She was wearing a turquoise sweater and pleated khaki pants. Her playing was awful but she looked so sweet, so unassuming, that I felt a new swell of love for her.

The television Betsy grew quickly. At first the episodes showed loveable things – Betsy putting a sunbonnet on her bulldog, Charlie, or Betsy trick-or-treating dressed as a skunk. But then they changed.

We sat on the floor of our apartment playing *Battleship* when her head played an episode of her putting her brother in an old refrigerator out in the backyard and laughing at the sound of his small fists pounding inside the door. After the knocking stopped she opened the door and he fell out, no longer conscious, and she shook him and shook him until he opened his eyes. She said, "You dare tell anyone and you're toast." Betsy'd tried turning the TV off then, but the television didn't do what we wanted it to.

I would have let it go if it was just that thing with her brother, but a few days later it showed her in a high school bathroom doing lines of cocaine before Calculus class and then in a bathroom at a party crying and plucking her eyelashes out with her fingertips in front of a mirror. I couldn't understand how this was Betsy, my Betsy, the untidy yet sensible woman I was about to marry. This Betsy was dark and hard, a lonesome planet of self-loathing. She was the type of woman Betsy and I made fun of together, mostly at Betsy's urging.

I didn't want to watch but couldn't help it and the next episode was Betsy driving home after a party, swerving down her sub-division, careening a station wagon back into the driveway. Headlights splashed against the garage door and Betsy shrieked upon seeing the bulldog in the drive just before hearing a *kahflunk* and the dog's yelp underneath tires. She screeched, got out of the car without putting it in park and the car rolled backwards into a neighbor's mailbox. By that time Betsy was down on the driveway holding the dog in her arms, its eyes full-pupilled and puzzled, viscera everywhere. Betsy scooped him up and ran into the house yelling to her mother and screaming Charlie! Charlie! Betsy's jeans were covered with blood and tufts of matted fur. She hung her television head as if to say, "Now you know me, Ray. Now you really know."

She got up and started to pack her clothes. I was on the couch with my knees pulled up to my chest; I needed something to separate us. On one of our first dates she said she didn't like dogs and I'd accepted it even though I'd wanted one because I thought some things were worth the sacrifice.

She rustled her shoes on and I heard the clink of the chain latch, the turn of the doorknob. Finally, I said, Wait! I told her to come back and to sit down. She turned away but I said, Please. Give it a minute.

I went to the closet and dug out my television -- the one with *Scooby Doo* that'd landed in my shopping cart that I'd nearly forgotten about. All that'd happened between us was because Betsy's television fell on her head and mine hadn't. So I plugged mine in and I sat next to Betsy, my fiancé, my beautiful, intelligent, soon-to-be wife, and I let her watch everything on my TV too so we would know, both of us, all the exquisite and awful versions of ourselves we'd been before that day.

KATRINA ROBERTS

THIS WAY to THE MUSEUM of RELIQUARIES

Where trembling leaves whorl up like a nest of black hair,
peppery strands pulled from worn tines
of her flat black brush. So many purple-brown hands
fallen silent beneath the leg of a pewter pachyderm --
the ancient copper beech under which I spent afternoons
whisper-chanting: nacreous, calamitous, nimbostratus.
Where else was I to store this all? (Pockets mostly
rent, earthenware cups crazed and seeping.) He followed
me home so I kept him.

Where light smears across an algaed bay, an ebb-tide
runs off with a porcelain dish sprigged the electric
blue of forget-me-nots, and a tiny tarnished spoon, raking
a jagged song I can only describe in terms of the fragrant
spell she dabbed precisely *here* behind one pink shell
of her cocked ear, *Eau de Toilette*, elegant, hounds-
toothed, and each peal of every miniscule
curlicued white bell chiming *lily, lily, lily-
of-the-valley.*

Where everyone was called out
of the churning black surf grown-
still, as a fleet of synchronized fins like a cloud's
glowering shadow, like Neolithic dorsal arrow-
heads (shot from beneath ponderous brine fathoms)
drifted by, dragging a fine net of silence in their wake.

Where even sweet moments of pooled warmth are
fraught. Our waxy honeycomb home, steadily dripping
honey despite an angry queen. And he, such a busy drone.

But a clean white swan birthed from crisp linen folds
might save me, might rest in my empty lap such that

I could lift a single soft thing to my lips (slick,
chapped), such that I could bury my scrubbed face

in spread wings asking nothing of me. The bunny-
shaped birthday cake flurried with a delicate snow of

coconut. A moth's filigreed frenulum trapped to become
a pendant, amber, pendulous around a stranger's stalk-

like neck. A stone-sized russet potato wrapped and baked
for hours in shiny foil to hold when my paws grow

cold during endless dark and serpentine rides on a train
to some distant ballet hall. A painted (emerald) wall

adorned with ornate sconces that reveal themselves (*no!*)
to be great fuzzed antlers -- sawed (*no!*) from once-

trumpeting, magnificent beasts; organs, pelts, hearts
long-tossed (though never truly lost, yes? *Tell*

me!) – like some enchanted Nordic prayer to love-
albeit-meted-out-in-angstroms, precise,

multi-fingered, tinkling, and eternally pointed skyward.

KATRINA ROBERTS

Scape

"So warm to night that Bats are flying near the Boats."
– JJ Audubon, 1821

Longing is the mind's silk, a trove
of treasures cast out and out
never to reach the burned-out
stars living still in our eyes.

That some animals come close
lets us catch our breaths –
their elegant paws, pleated wings.

You're getting warm, he sang
before streaming off again
into shadows.

One might wonder
whether it all
had been worth it.

Oh, how often
I've been
wrong.

KATRINA ROBERTS

Bolt

Her wings rose in my chest
and fell
because she felt a chill
in the wind
and feared there wasn't time.

Truth is
there would have been
no better minute
to float and wrap ourselves
together within

a length of silk
unfurled
from the teal bolt of sky
lying in wait
stilly above us, to become.

Then he scissored
his legs
making the moment flee
dashing what
hope there might have been.

KATRINA ROBERTS

A Word Like Amplitude

I've been bridesmaid to the creek-bed several times.
Watched blonde children skip across a fallen trunk
as though they'll never die.
Made a bonfire spring to life from a single molten tear
and twigs, to lick the spacious sky.

I've been stilled for a cool instant by a storm
of words meant for another restless girl with more
precious pelt than mine, a finer hide.

That rare red fox might as well be my heart.
She knows the pure transfixion of untrammeled snow.
She scatters a fist of torn petals from something
as fragile as a poppy, and carries on.

Night often finds me hopping between cool stones
of each *what if*, but never scolds. Night fixes me
with a distant planet's wink, then leaves me not exactly
cold, but confused. How old you seemed, though
I'm more ancient than you'll ever be.
You played me like a string. Since
you took away our toy so long ago, we sing
no more for you. What portents did we miss
among letters you let slip, each a scrap of bark

you floated down desire's stream, weaving its thunder-
hued trail through banks fronded with fiddleheads?

Days I've spent scavenging 13.7 billion candles
so the universe might have a festive cake.
Praise the broken thing. The way

the dead finch rose as though to fly
for maggots writhing inside. Happy birthday, boy-
oh-boy. You certainly left us chilled by the iceberg-
blue of your gaze. How long you sat, pale and still against
the pale and stiller porcelain, before the blooming
began...? Before your son arrived at his appointed hour
to find a door ajar, to peer into the wrong
answer of your much-too-quiet tiled room, stunned?

You must have known a particulate wonder, a tingeing
like tea as some monstrous weight drained out
in feathered spools. How dark the water had grown for us
to come upon, how ruddy and smeared,
like some epic rosy-fingered dawn gone entirely awry.

LAURA READ

Mary's Waking Dream

What English teacher doesn't love to tell it?
Sometimes I forget my students are there. Sometimes
a flock of black birds flies past the classroom window.

In my version, Mary was looking out the kitchen
window, her hands in the sink, the rain
sliding down the glass in rivulets.

"It proved a wet, ungenial summer," Mary wrote in 1816.
She wasn't even in the room when the men came up
with the idea. Who can write the best ghost story?

For days nothing came to Mary. Byron wrote,
"Began my ghost story after tea. Twelve o'clock,
really began to talk ghostly." It's October here

and I plan to talk ghostly as much as I can.
Like this: Byron said Shelley ran screaming into the room
where he was writing. They had to give him ether.

He had seen a woman whose nipples were eyes.
My favorite piece of art is Man Ray's *Indestructible Object*,
a photograph of Lee Miller's eye that he affixed

to a metronome. For years I felt that way about someone.
It was hard to do anything. I've been to Switzerland.
When the train pulled into the station, the sky

in the Alps was pink and the snow held its glow
like a heart. I was with that boy then.
It's almost been 200 years since Frankenstein

and his monster came to Mary in a dream.
Then she hardly slept. She could see how the pieces
of skin didn't quite stick, how the Creature had to drag

his too-big body around, how he stood outside
that family's cottage and learned to read and speak
and finally revealed himself to them, but of course

they were frightened. When one of my students tells me
she didn't like *Frankenstein*, I am incredulous.
Doesn't she know that in 2011 the astronomer

Donald Olson visited Lake Geneva to find out
the exact time of Mary's "waking dream"?
It happened between 2 and 3 a.m. on the 16th of June,

1816. I can't believe the stars can tell us this.
Mary lost her feminist mother at birth.
Then she lost four of her five children and then

Percy in the ocean. But one night she woke up
knowing that if we create something, it will always
belong to us. Its small wand will swing back

and forth inside you, ticking, until you want
to break it. And if it leaves, you'll have to
wander the icy North until it's found.

LAURA READ

You Have to Fight Magic with Magic

When it rains, my hair springs
into snakes. I have to hide
from myself. And everyone I look at
turns to stone. I used to look away
when someone was walking towards me
down a hall. Maybe I already knew
who I was. Zeus can rape anyone
and it's just a small part of the story.
And Poseidon everyone loves.
For brushing our skin with salt.
For bringing the sea so close
and then taking it back.
But I didn't say yes. Of course,
I used to be beautiful. Of course,
it was my fault the ocean wanted me.
How many women can it swallow,
in myth and in the real wind,
some with stones in their pockets?
I have to hold onto my hair, grabbing
big clumps, trying to keep it down.
I only want to talk to someone
without breaking. There is me
and the myth of me. Just like you.
You are the roar in the blood.
You are what love could have been.
And now all I can do is keep walking
the edge of this ocean.

CONTRIBUTORS

Zan Agzigian is a poet, story writer and playwright with an MFA in Fiction from EWU. She lives in Vinegar Flats, Spokane, with her dog, Itzy, and is host/producer of a weekly Sunday eclectic music hour, *Soundspace*, on Spokane Public Radio.

David Alasdair earned an MFA from Eastern Washington University and has seen the Loch Ness Monster.

Terry Bain is the author of *You Are a Dog* and *We Are the Cat*. He lives in Spokane with his wife and three kids, one dog, two cats, and a bearded dragon. He can be found on the web at terrybain.com.

Elissa Ball is a feminist performance poet and professional Tarot reader who lives in Spokane, WA. In 2012, Blue Begonia Press published *The Punks Are Writing Love Songs*, Elissa's debut book of poems. Follow her on Twitter @ElissaBall.

Sheri Boggs is the Youth Collection Development Librarian for the Spokane County Library District. She's worked as a bookseller, librarian, editor and writer, and currently spins stories from her 1940s era house on the South Hill.

Marcus Brown is an artist living in Spokane with a small clan of cats and a large collection of dolls that he keeps telling everyone are "Action Figures". Japanese folklore and the mythical creatures found within have long been an interest of Marcus', so he jumped at the chance to collaborate on a Kappa-centric tale with the talented Keely Honeywell.

Polly Buckingham's collection *The Expense of a View* won the Katherine Anne Porter Prize in Short Fiction (due out Nov 2016), and her chapbook *A Year of Silence* won the Jeanne Leiby Memorial Chapbook Award for Fiction (2013). Polly is founding editor of StringTown Press and teaches creative writing at Eastern Washington University. Her work appears in *The Gettysburg Review*, *The Threepenny Review* and elsewhere.

Ben Cartwright grew up in Spokane, moved away, stayed away for a long time, and now is back. His fiction has appeared in *Johnny America*, and *The Stinging Fly's International Flash Fiction Showcase*. He teaches at Spokane Falls Community College, and his favorite mythical beast is student loan forgiveness.

Meagan Ciesla's fiction and nonfiction have appeared in *Kenyon Review*, *Cimarron Review*, *The Long Story*, and other publications. She holds a PhD from University of Missouri and teaches at Gonzaga University.

Ann M. Colford was destined for a life in words thanks to growing up in a town called Reading, near Boston. After a long detour into the world of numbers, she spent 10 years herding words for the Inlander. She now scribbles lines and counts beans on Spokane's lower South Hill under the supervision of her feline companions.

Chris Cook's poetry collection, *The View from the Broken Mic*, came out in 2012. His new book, *Damn Good Cookie*, is due out in 2016 from Korrektiv Press. He is happily married to his wife Kathi, who is not a monster.

Elizabeth Kaye Cook is an MFA Fiction candidate at the Inland Northwest Center for Writers. Her work has been published in various online and print journals such as *Ruminate* and *Sixfold*. She currently serves as Co-Fiction Editor of *Willow Springs*.

Beth Cooley has published poetry, fiction and non-fiction in a number of journals and anthologies, as well as two YA novels with Delacorte Press. She teaches at Gonzaga University and enjoys spending time with horses.

Kris Dinnison lives and writes in Spokane, Washington. Her first novel, *You and Me and Him*, was released in July 2015 from Houghton Mifflin Harcourt.

Scott Eubanks moved to Spokane in 2004. Since then, he has lived on the South Hill and in North Central, East Valley and West Central. His work has appeared in *Memoir* (and), *The Whitefish Review*, and *Zone 3*.

Eli Francovich is a journalist and writer who struggles to remember that process is far more important than product.

Henrietta Goodman is the author of *Take What You Want* (Beatrice Hawley Award, Alice James Books, 2007) and *Hungry Moon* (Mountain West Poetry Series, 2013). She teaches at the University of Montana and is co-coordinator of the Open Country Reading Series in Missoula.

Tim Greenup's poems have appeared or are forthcoming in *Redivider*, *LEVELER*, *BOAAT*, and elsewhere. He teaches English at Spokane Falls Community College.

Ginger Grey received her MFA from Eastern Washington University and has been published in various places (most recently *Terrain.org* and *The Georgetown Review*). She teaches at Gonzaga University.

Emily Gwinn lives with her family in Spokane. She is the Assistant Executive Director for the LiTFUSE literary workshop and an editor for the upcoming collection of poetry on motherhood, *All We Can Hold*.

Vanessa Lea Halls likes walking her dog, playing *World of Warcraft*, and talking nonsense. She lives in Spokane.

Elin Hawkinson is a second-year MFA candidate in fiction at The Inland Northwest Center for Writers. Her work has appeared in *Midwestern Gothic* and *The Inquisitive Eater*, among others.

Dennis Held has published two books of poetry: *Betting on the Night*, and *Ourself*.

Keely Honeywell is a writer of stories and to-do lists, as well as a designer, and programmer.

M. Hunt is a Spokane writer whose short stories and essays have appeared in *YA Review Network* (YARN), *Cricket Magazine*, *Parents Magazine* and newspapers throughout the Oregon and Washington. She is a finalist for the Katherine Paterson prize given by *Hunger Mountain: The VCFA Journal of the Arts*, and a winner of the *Pacific Northwest Inlander*'s short-fiction award.

Ceilan Hunter-Green is a graduate of Gonzaga University who now works as a barista, printmaker, writer, zine editor, proofreader and know-it-all.

Kim Kent lives in Spokane, WA, where she is an MFA candidate at the Inland Northwest Center for Writers. She enjoys talking with her hands, small spaces, and the word trampoline.

Amaris Feland Ketcham has work published in *Los Angeles Review*, *Rattle*, and *Utne Reader*, among others. She also has an essay and poems forthcoming in *Creative Nonfiction* and *Kenyon Review*.

Leyna Krow is the author of the forthcoming short story collection *I'm Fine, But You Appear to Be Sinking* (Featherproof Books, 2016). She has an MFA from Eastern Washington University. She lives in Spokane's Garland District with her husband, a dog, and several house plants.

Yvonne Higgins Leach is the author of *Another Autumn* (WordTech Editions, 2014). She earned a Master of Fine Arts from Eastern Washington University in 1986. She has spent decades balancing a career in communications and public relations, raising a family, and pursuing her love of writing poetry. For more information, visit www.yvonnehigginsleach.com.

J. Robert Lennon's nine books include the novels *Mailman* and *Familiar*, and the story collections *Pieces for the Left Hand* and *See You in Paradise*. He lives in Ithaca, New York.

Amy Silbernagel McCaffree is a senior writer for *Out There Monthly* magazine and teaches writing for Spokane Community College. She calls Spokane home along with her outdoorsy, non-monster husband and their two children. She has a MFA in poetry from Eastern Washington University and her work has appeared in *Rock and Sling*, *Railtown Almanac*, *Northwest Runner*, and *Labyrinth*.

Elisabeth Sharp McKetta teaches writing for Harvard Extension School and is the author of three books, *The Fairy Tales Mammals Tell* (2013), *The Creative Year: 52 Workshops for Writers* (2014), and *Poetry for Strangers* (2015). Her PhD (Univ. Texas 2009) focused on the intersections between fairy tales and autobiography. She lives in Boise with her family. See more online at www.elisabethsharpmcketta.com.

Darcy McMurtery cut her teeth on folklore and fiction. When she's not writing, she works as a teen services librarian in the Seattle area. She recently published her first chapbook, *Feast of Needs*.

Claire McQuerry's poetry collection *Lacemakers* won the Crab Orchard First Book Prize. Her poems have appeared in *Poetry Northwest*, *Western Humanities Review*, *American Literary Review*, and other journals. She teaches at Whitworth University.

Simeon Mills is a writer, cartoonist, and teacher in Spokane. His graphic novel, *Butcher Paper*, was published by Scablands Books.

Karen Munro lives and writes in Portland, OR. She is married to a wonderful monster.

Hannah Faith Notess won the Michael Waters Poetry Prize for her first collection of poems, *The Multitude*, from Southern Indiana Review Press. She is the editor of Seattle Pacific University's *Response Magazine* and of *Jesus Girls: True Tales of Growing Up Female and Evangelical*, a collection of personal essays. She lives in Seattle.

Stephanie Oakes' debut novel, *The Sacred Lies of Minnow Bly*, was released from Dial/Penguin in 2015. She is a library media specialist and teacher in Spokane, Washington.

Raised in Tennessee, Audrey Duff Overstreet was a reporter for *The American Lawyer* magazine in New York City before relocating to Austin, Texas where she wrote about the live music scene for the *Austin American-Statesman* and was Politics Editor for the *Austin Chronicle*. She enjoyed her subsequent adventures as a Press Secretary on Capitol Hill for two U.S. Congressmen, but her journey to Spokane and work as the former Marketing Director of the Spokane Symphony have been her best moves yet.

Amy Ratto Parks is the author of *Bread and Water Body* (2004), *Song of Days, Torn and Mended* (2014), and *Radial Bloom* (2017). She teaches writing at the University of Montana.

Natalie Peeterse has an MFA from the University of Montana. Her chapbook *Black Birds : Blue Horse, An Elegy* won the Gold Line Press Poetry Prize in 2011. She lives in Missoula, MT where she coordinates the Open Country Reading Series.

Kate Peterson earned her MFA from Eastern Washington University in Spokane, where she now teaches composition. Her poems have been published in *Sugar House Review*, *Baldhip*, *The Sierra Nevada Review*, *Hawaii Pacific Review*, and *Glassworks* among others. Links to more work can be found at www.katelaurenpeterson.tumblr.com.

Kristina Pfleegor is a writing tutor and teacher. Originally from Portland, Oregon, she has spent parts of her life in Kenya, Minnesota, Hawai'i, and eastern Washington. She holds an MFA in creative writing from Eastern Washington University, and her poems appear in *Rock & Sling*, *ASCENT*, *Bluestem*, and other journals.

Shann Ray grew up in Montana. A National Endowment for the Arts Fellow, his poetry and prose have been honored with the American Book Award, the High Plains Book Award, and the Bakeless Prize. Because of his wife and three daughters, he believes in love.

Laura Read's chapbook *The Chewbacca on Hollywood Boulevard Reminds Me of You* was published by Floating Bridge Press in 2010, and her collection *Instructions for My Mother's Funeral* was published in 2012 by the University of Pittsburgh Press. She teaches English at Spokane Falls Community College and is Spokane's current Poet Laureate.

Katrina Roberts has published four books of poems: *Underdog; Friendly Fire; The Quick;* and *How Late Desire Looks;* and edited the anthology: *Because You Asked: A Book of Answers on the Art & Craft of the Writing Life.* She teaches at Whitman College, curates the Visiting Writers Reading Series, and co-founded and operates the Walla Walla Distilling Company.

Julia Rox is currently pursuing her MFA in poetry at Eastern Washington University. She recently moved to Spokane from Nashville, TN, where she graduated from Lipscomb University with a BA in English and philosophy. She loves dogs with long bodies and short legs.

Marianne Salina lives in Spokane, Washington where she writes and makes things out of paper and sticks. She received her MFA from Eastern Washington University and some of her work may be found in *Birkensnake*, *The Adirondack Review*, *Split Lip Magazine*, *Word Riot*, and various other online publications.

Ryan Scariano's chapbook, *Smithereens*, was published by Imperfect Press, in 2013. Currently, he lives in Spokane and adjuncts at Eastern Washington University. Learn more at ryanscariano.com.

Siobhán Scarry is the author of the poetry collection *Pilgrimly* (Parlor Press, 2014). She is currently Chair of the Literary Studies Department at Bethel College, Kansas, where she teaches literature & creative writing and serves as faculty mentor to the undergraduate literary magazine *Yawp!*

Karin Schalm has published work in *Camas*, *CutBank*, *The Sun* and other journals. She earned an MFA in Poetry, an MA in Literature, and an MS in Environmental Studies from the University of Montana, where she currently serves as the Creative Writing Program Coordinator.

Kisha Lewellyn Schlegel holds an MS in Environmental Studies from the University of Montana and an MFA from Iowa's Nonfiction Writing Program. She has published essays in *The Kenyon Review Online*, *Conjunctions*, *The Iowa Review* and elsewhere. A recent recipient of an Artist Trust grant, she teaches creative writing at Whitman College.

Rob Schlegel is the author of *The Lesser Fields* (Center for Literary Publishing, 2009) and *January Machine* (Four Way Books, 2014). With the poet Daniel Poppick, he co-edits *The Catenary Press*.

Nicole Sheets teaches at Whitworth University, lives in West Central, and tweets @heynicolesheets.

Jordan Smith-Zodrow graduated from Seattle Pacific University with a BA in English. Her poetry has appeared in *RiverLit* and *Potluck Magazine*. She can be reached at jsmithzodrow@gmail.com.

Rachel Toor's next book, *Misunderstood: Why the Humble Rat May Be Your Best Pet Ever*, will be published in June by Farrar, Straus and Giroux. She teaches in the MFA program at EWU and is mother to Helen, a brilliant and athletic 50-pound mutt.

Lareign Ward received an MFA in Creative Nonfiction from Eastern Washington University. Prior work has appeared in *Big Lucks* and *Trop*. A native of Texas, she currently lives and works in Spokane.

Matthew Weaver is a Spokane native and playwright. Plays include *Bed Ride, Gluttony and Lust are Friends, Aces Are Feverish,* and shorter plays, *Feminine Care, The Girl Wore Red Licorice,* among others.

Ellen Welcker is a poet in Spokane. More on her writing at ewelcker.tumblr.com.

Maya Jewell Zeller is the author of the poetry collections *Yesterday, the Bees* and *Rust Fish,* and of individual essays and poems, published widely. She also edits fiction for *Crab Creek Review,* co-directs the Beacon Hill Reading Series, and teaches writing at Gonzaga University and online through other colleges. Maya lives north of Spokane with her husband and their two children. Learn more at mayajewellzeller.com.

ACKNOWLEDGMENTS

Scablands Lit would like to thank the following individuals and organizations for making this second Lilac City Fairy Tales anthology possible:

Our diligent volunteer editors, including Anastasia Hilton, Melissa Huggins, and Ceilan Hunter-Green

Our intrepid designer, Keely Honeywell

Writer and professor Beth Cooley for her eagle-eye in editing the galleys

Our ever friendly and hard-working printer Russ Davis with Gray Dog Press

Our talented cover designer John Rawley, who was also so helpful as Marketing Director for the Bing

The Friends of the Bing

Passionate arts supporters Jerry and Patty Dicker, who are always seeking vibrant events to bring to Spokane

The compassionate and beautifully organized Brooke Matson of INK Art Space

The Inland and Pacific Northwest's community of writers, both those who appear in the anthology and those who do not. Keep writing, everyone!

Our euphonious musicians for the February 14th event, Liz Rognes and Windoe's Karli Ingersoll

INK Art Space for great programming for literacy and arts.

For more information
INK Art Space: inkspokane.org
Scablands Lit: scablands-lit.org
The Friends of the Bing: friendsofthebing.org
Liz Rognes: lizrognes.com
Windoe: windoe.bandcamp.com